D1710619

QUALITY FACILITY MANAGEMENT

QUALITY
FACILITY MANAGEMENT
A MARKETING AND CUSTOMER SERVICE
APPROACH

Stormy Friday
David G. Cotts

John Wiley & Sons, Inc.
New York • Chichester • Brisbane • Toronto • Singapore

Library of Congress Cataloging in Publication Data:

Friday, Stormy, 1947-
    Quality facility management : a marketing and customer service
  approach / Stormy Friday, David G. Cotts.
        p.   cm.
  Includes bibliographical references and index.
  ISBN 0-471-02322-1 (cloth)
    1. Facility management.   2. Total quality management.   3. Consumer
  satisfaction. I. Cotts, David G. II. Title.
  HD1394.F75   1995
  658.5'62–dc20   94-21164

Printed in the United States of America

10 9 8 7 6 5

This book is dedicated to the people dearest to me who have supported my concept of facility management consulting from a time when they couldn't explain what it meant to the firm's present day success. Without the steadfast support, reinforcement and encouragement of my parents, Margaret and Durant Friday and my husband Kit Bradley, the dream of providing technical assistance to my fellow facility colleagues would not have come to fruition. My way of thanking them is to publicly recognize and share their contribution with you.

S.F.

To the F-106 Gang who always did it with quality....
the old fashioned way.

D.G.C.

CONTENTS

ʾ

List of Figures

PREFACE

The impetus for this book came from our belief that facility managers everywhere continue to be the true unsung quality heroes of our companies and agencies. Through the efforts of these highly professional and skilled individuals, who toil in often thankless, anxiety-prone and contentious environments, somehow billions of square feet of buildings worldwide are planned, maintained and operated each day.

Facility managers are the quiet heros of companies and agencies.

"But where is the tie to quality?" you might ask. "What qualifies us to be considered knowledgeable with respect to quality?" Well, any facility manager worth his/her caulk has seen quality in action, particularly on the most difficult of days. Do many other professionals have to rise at the crack of dawn to stand with a stopwatch by elevator banks and time passenger cars because the CFO wants to know if they are meeting the passenger delivery times guaranteed by the manufacturer? Or, do they walk into their offices in the wee hours of the morning after being up all night handling a bomb threat only to find a shoe box filled with dead roaches and mice — a present from a disgruntled employee? The last time a top executive gave you a one hour dissertation on the art of dusting and vacuuming an executive office suite, you better believe you had new respect for what lies behind the definition of quality.

The tie to quality is that we see it in action each and every day.

Most facility managers are responsible for a litany of activities, which range from worrying about the temperature in buildings and seeing that each and every employee has parked his/her car in the appropriate space, to overseeing the design and construction of major facility complexes. On the one hand the job requires the complex and specialized skills necessary to manage some of the most sophisticated technologies, while on the other hand, it includes such mundane details as ensuring that the rest rooms have an adequate supply of paper towels!

Common denominator is the customer.

How does this relate to quality? The common denominator is the customer. In case after case, situation after situation, the *customer* determines what quality is; the customer's satisfaction level determines whether the facility management (hereafter referred to as FM) organization is successful.

If you accept then, that the above qualifies facility professionals to be counted among those who *know* about quality, what makes us believe that you are *silent* practitioners? You only have to search library and bookstore shelves, and on-line reference libraries to see that major works on quality FM are conspicuously absent. With so much "practice" material on FM, why are there no books on quality FM? For those of you in the business, the answer is obvious. You are all so busy planning, managing and operating those buildings that you don't have time to talk and write about what you know on the subject of quality.

This book is one perspective on quality FM.

For these reasons, we have taken up the cause. We are well aware that this book is not the definitive word on quality FM. We didn't intend it to be and hope it will not be misjudged by those who are expecting a more scholarly work on the subject. This book is one perspective on quality FM, but one we know others in our profession share. As both pioneering practitioners in the FM business and ongoing consultants to our colleagues, we have hands-on experience with quality FM and wanted to talk about it. Our book is here not only to promote some "how-to's" of quality FM, but also to document FM examples which demonstrate that your compatriots have gone about their work in a quality fashion, without much fanfare or recognition.

We salute facility managers everywhere!

STORMY FRIDAY

DAVID G. COTTS

Acknowledgments

We would like to express our sincere gratitude to our wonderful colleagues who provided Best Practices for our Chapter Six. Their practices serve to reinforce our concepts about quality facility management and we appreciate their willingness to share their experiences with you. Our Best Practice contributors include, in the order in which they appear in Chapter Six:

- Barry Yach – Section Manager, Property Management, Bell Canada;
- Frank Yockey – Quality/Productivity Manager, Hewlett-Packard;
- Dan Nordmark – Facilities Manager, Boeing Defense & Space Group;
- Thomas F. Doherty – Manager, Strategic Planning, Bell Atlantic Network Services Incorporated;
- Jaan Meri – Manager, Facilities Engineering and Operations, Celestica Inc.;
- James E. Loesch – Chief Facilities Engineer, Johns Hopkins University Applied Physics Laboratory;
- Linda L. Flaherty – Engineering Planning Specialist, Lockheed Missiles & Space Company, Inc.;
- Charles Collins – Regional Manager, Landis & Gyr Powers, Inc.;
- Fred J. Klammt – Aptek Associates;
- Francene M. Edeson – Manager of Regional Building Services, Southern California Edison; and

- Gayle Silva – Project Administrator, Information Resources Management Service, General Services Administration.

We also are indebted to Clorinda Haug of Create 'n Image, who designed and produced the layout and graphics, as well as converted our difficult text into the final, readable product. She tirelessly worked and reworked chapters for us as we added and deleted materials, and without her patience and technical skill, this book would not have been possible.

Introduction

The Authors' Perspective on Quality FM: Why Did We Do It?

Few of us would debate the point that over the last five years the international business community has witnessed a movement so dramatic in its widespread acceptance and implementation that virtually all organizations have incorporated all or part of its doctrines. We are speaking, of course, about the quality movement. So why then did we feel compelled to write yet another book on quality? Why did we do it?

Writing a book is difficult; collaborating on one often can be disastrous, but in this instance we brought compatible backgrounds and experiences to the task. This book, we hope, is an example of the best that comes from joint authorship. While we approach the subject of quality in FM from quite different perspectives, we found that our philosophies were quite similar. Both of us have been practicing facility managers. One of us currently is an entrepreneur who specializes in advising facility organizations on customer service; the other is a facility manager of long-standing who still practices what he preaches. When we put the two together we thought we could offer some insight into quality FM which heretofore has not been documented.

What do you get when you cross an entrepreneur with a practitioner?

A helpful book on FM, we hope!

The Old-Fashioned Way

Over the course of two years, as we both participated in the International Facility Management Association (IFMA) Focus Group on Continuous Improvement in FM and heard the discussions taking place, we found that we shared more than the Nation's Capitol as our home base. While both of us felt naturally drawn to the quality movement and its basic principles, we had reservations about the possibility of formal Total Quality Management (TQM) being implemented widely by the broad range of facility managers that we knew. In a time of increasing cost consciousness on the part of facility managers, most highly structured, formal TQM efforts we were hearing about required dollar and staff resource commitments which went way beyond what many facility managers had available. The question we then raised was, if you do not implement a full TQM program, does this mean there isn't anything you can do about quality FM?

As we talked, we found we agreed that certain principles from the quality movement were essential to good FM regardless of what it is called. We also agreed that those principles, all of which start from the base of customer service, had been present wherever we had seen good FM long before the recent emphasis on TQM. For that reason, we decided that what we really wanted to write about was quality management of facilities...the old-fashioned way.

Quality FM does not necessarily equate to a full TQM program.

Here's to You!

Hopefully this book will be as applicable to you, the Office Manager who has FM as an ancillary duty, as to you, the Vice President of Facilities for a Fortune 100 company. We have consciously tried to make this as applicable for the Director of Facilities for the state of Montana as for the project manager of an outsourcing firm providing all facilities services to a corporation. Since the authors bring a broad range of experience to

We hope this book is useful to all types of facility managers.

this task, we have tried to be all inclusive in targeting our audience. We believe that what we say is applicable to all of you involved in FM regardless of whether you are in the public or private sector, part of an in-house organization or a contracted firm, working within large facilities or small ones, or in leased spaced versus owned. We think you will be able to relate to our approach to quality management of facilities and the tools and techniques we recommend you try.

WHAT IS THIS THING CALLED QUALITY?

For purposes of this book when we speak of quality, we mean more than "superiority in kind."[1] Quality to us needs to be part of the very fabric of a facility organization. It has to be deep-seated in the values and culture of the organization and should be pervasive throughout all levels. Quality to us is indicated by observable conditions within a facility organization:

- When all members of the department, including all of the contractors, view themselves as totally responsible for the entire facility, not just their specialty, and they are empowered to make decisions and corrections. FEELING THAT "IT'S MY JOB!"

Get the "It's My Job Feeling!"

- When there is dedication to producing the absolutely best service within the resource limitations set. DOING IT RIGHT THE FIRST TIME!

Do it right the first time.

- When effectiveness and appropriateness of service drive the service delivery system. MEETING THE SERVICE NEEDS OF CUSTOMERS!

OUR FIVE PILLARS OF QUALITY

To achieve the kind of quality FM we are striving for throughout this book, our experience indicates that you should be governed by five principles or themes:

1. Quality services start with customer service. Only the customer will define whether you are performing the right service and how well you are doing it. THE

Meet the service needs of customers.

CUSTOMER DRIVES THE PROCESS!

2. You must be committed to continual improvement. THERE IS NO SHORT-TERM SOLUTION!

3. You must be willing (and able) to measure and be measured. BENCHMARKING AND METRICS ARE ESSENTIAL!

4. Employees must be empowered, must be held responsible, and must view themselves and their jobs within a broad context. THE FRONT LINE SERVICE WORKER SHOULD HAVE FLEXIBILITY TO MAKE DECISIONS WITH THE CUSTOMER!

5. Quality service should be both recognized and marketed inside and outside the company. THERE IS NO SUCH THING AS MARKETING BY SIO (SITTING IN YOUR OFFICE)!

The customer drives the process

There is no short-term solution.

Benchmark and use metrics.

Empower your FM staff.

Marketing ≠ SIO!

WHAT'S DRIVING US AND WHO'S IN THE DRIVER'S SEAT WITH QUALITY?

Total Quality Management has been a "hot" topic in FM for about the last five years, driven by your need to do more with less and by your companies' needs to become increasingly competitive in an international marketplace. For many organizations quality has become a pseudonym for national and international competitions like the Baldridge award. In some of the larger companies, over the last several years, we have seen some of your colleagues become the executive charged with quality within their organization. We suspect that stems from the fact that any facility manager not oriented to customer service does not last long and one who is successful in this area can make an easy transition from FM to quality management. We cannot ignore that TQM has been a major management initiative for some organizations.

WHILE TQM IS HOT, THIS BOOK IS NOT JUST ABOUT TQM

Having said all that, however, we still are doubtful that most facility managers will implement a full-blown Total Quality program. First of all, facility managers in smaller organizations simply lack the resources to field an organized program. TQM programs are both dollar and personnel intensive, and facility managers in smaller organizations already have a full plate of activities. Secondly, we are already receiving some negative feedback on the wisdom of a formalized TQM program, particularly among some Baldridge award winners.[2] Finally some find the concept of a TQM program daunting, even scary.

TQM may not be right for all companies and agencies.

Your authors have *always* thought that quality management and FM went well together, regardless of what name it was given. So whether you are a skeptic, a non-believer, or an advocate for Total Quality Management, this book is for you. It is also for those "in between folks" among which we would both number ourselves. Our goal is to help you grasp what we consider the real principles of quality and help you apply them. Along the way, we have attempted to provide some basic guidelines, checklists, and "how to's" to make the process easier.

Our goal is to help you with the principles of quality.

QUALITY IS AN INTEGRAL PART OF THE TOTAL PRACTICE OF FM!

While our book focuses on five governing principles of quality, we want to stress how important we feel it is to embrace quality in all areas of facility practice. Each facility manager reading this book manages a slightly different "menu" of services. As a way for you to incorporate quality into the very core of FM, when you think of quality, we recommend that you consider how you will PLAN for quality, ORGANIZE for quality, STAFF for quality, DIRECT for quality, and EVALU-

Quality management and FM were made for each other.

ATE the effect of quality as you apply these principles to each of the functions of FM. Our principles are as valid to the functions of the mail room as they are in project management, as useful for a strategic planning group as for the custodial crew.

USE US!

You will find some humor, but the message is serious.

We trust that you will find this book easy to read and easy to use. It is intended to be just what it appears to be, a desk side reference where you can easily find the topic that interests you. We have made margin notes to use both as ready references and to provide you with some "jewels" on the topic of quality. We have intentionally written with a light tone, sometimes even tongue-in-cheek, and have sprinkled in some humor. We hope you will appreciate our efforts to make the book enjoyable, and realize, at the same time, that the message is dead serious, because it is. The provision of quality services, as defined by the customer, will, more than any other factor, determine the success or failure of a facility manager. We see quality FM as the only way to do business.

END NOTES

1. *Websters' New Collegiate Dictionary*, Eighth Edition, p. 936.
2. Scott Madison Paton, "Is TQM Dead?," *Quality Digest*, April 1994, p. 24.

CHAPTER 1

QUALITY AND CUSTOMER SERVICE ARE SYNONYMOUS WITH FM

THE OLD-FASHIONED DEFINITION OF QUALITY FM

First, we need to clear the air. Some of you might question our use of "the old-fashioned way" in defining quality FM. "These are the 90's," people said to us, "You need to be sending the message that we are high-tech experts and efficient business leaders who are in tune with what is happening in the industry. Old-fashioned implies out-of-date and antiquated and that is the last message we want to send."

Does "old-fashioned" imply antiquated?

These statements confirm the old "glass is half empty or half full" theory. It all depends on your viewpoint. The term old-fashioned has two distinct interpretations. Either you view it negatively or it seems to imply core values. Instead of considering this viewpoint as passé, to us old-fashioned means returning to the way we learned to do things in years past. For many facility managers that learning experience was very positive.

Viewpoint is the key. "Old-fashioned" can mean reflecting on principles we learned about FM years ago.

As it applies to quality management of facilities, from our perspective, old-fashioned means looking at the provision of facility services the way we were taught to do, long before anyone packaged the terms "quality" and "quality management" and delivered them to us as if they were new commodities on the market. Quality

Quality FM is not new, just because we may focus on something called TQM.

FM is not new. What we have been led to believe, however, is that we must learn a whole *new* set of doctrines, a whole *new* set of buzzwords, and brand *new* measurements in order to be "90's-smart" when it comes to quality. To a certain extent we have been taken in by the "spin doctors"[1] who have tried to tell us that what we used to know about quality is now out-of-date. If the current TQM gurus had asked us, we could have told them a great deal about quality. While we need to be open to new techniques for communicating with customers and measuring the effectiveness and efficiency of service delivery, we also need to reinforce what already works.

GETTING BACK TO BASICS: THE CUSTOMER DRIVES THE PROCESS

First Pillar of Quality: The customer is the true judge of the quality process and outcome.

We have all said at one time or another, "Being in the facilities business would be a great job, if only we didn't have to deal with customers." Unfortunately, all too often, facility managers really do feel this way and have a tendency to pay lip service to the value placed on the customer. Our underlying premise, and one of our five pillars of quality, is that the customer drives the facility services process and defines quality. This is not particularly startling or revelatory as it is fundamental to sound management and marketing practice in general, but it must be a firm belief on the part of facility managers as we feel it goes to the very core of quality facility services. The concept that customers are the real judges of what constitutes quality in terms of the service process, as well as the service outcome, is one which facility managers need to endorse wholeheartedly. Perhaps each of you should hang a sign on your walls which reads "The customer, and only the customer, defines the quality of our services." Your job depends on it!

IDENTIFYING YOUR CUSTOMERS

If you agree that your customers play an important role in defining the quality of your service process and service outcome, then you must be certain that you fully understand your customer population. You probably think your staff are knowledgeable about who your customers are, but you might be surprised about their lack of knowledge if you ask them to define the customers of your services. At your next staff meeting, take a few minutes and have your management team complete the following exercise. You want to leave the instructions vague in order to see how each staff member defines "categories and customers."

Most FM organizations truly do not know their customers. How knowledgeable are you?

FIGURE 1.1

DEFINING CUSTOMERS

Identify by category, all customers of the facility organization.

Category	*Customer*
1. _____	_____
	_____
	_____
2. _____	_____
	_____
	_____
3. _____	_____
	_____
	_____
	_____
4. _____	_____

Can you name at least nine categories of customers?

It has been our experience that most facility organizations inconsistently identify who their customers are. Typically, one or more categories of customers is missing from the list. If your staff is not able to identify at least four of the categories of customers delineated below, they do not have a full grasp of your customer population. At a minimum, your management team should have identified:

1. Customers by organization unit

Depending on the way in which you are organized to deliver facility services, your management team should have identified customers of organizational units. They may see customers on a departmental basis such as finance, human resources, research, manufacturing, information systems or marketing.

2. Customers by building unit

You may be organized to provide service on a facility basis in addition to or instead of by organizational unit. You may have organizational units in whole or in part in different buildings, in leased and in owned facilities and your staff may see customers in terms of building populations. Customer service in a leased facility where you do not control all the FM related activities is much different than in an owned one.

3. Customers by business unit

Perhaps your company is organized along business unit lines as discrete cost centers. These may be different than traditional organization chart units and may be the way in which you identify a customer population.

4. Staff of the facility organization

If your senior staff have not identified each other as internal customers, they have made a grievous error. Consider that if you, the facility manager, placed each and every member of your staff out in the parking lot with a desk and telephone and told them to provide facility services by themselves, they would be hard pressed to do so. We find on a regular basis that facility organizations forget that we ourselves are internal customers and need to take the facility organization staff into account when we consider our service delivery systems. We need each other to provide facility services and have to be cognizant of that fact when we talk about customer service.

5. *Top management*

With any luck, your group is way ahead of us when it comes to identifying customers. Top management is a customer category which needs to be addressed as a separate entity. As we will discuss in our next section, top management is a discrete customer population which has service needs and delivery requirements that differ from other customer populations.

6. *External clients of 1, 2 and 3 and visitors*

Each and every one of the above internal customers has an external customer base. In many cases, these external customers have special relationships with your internal customers and you need to know about them and how they affect the delivery of your services to the primary customer.

7. *External vendors to the facility organization*

External vendors are becoming more and more important to us as customers as we think of them as "partners" in the provision of service to our internal customers. As partners, vendors should share the same values and beliefs with respect to our internal customers as the facility organization staff. It should not make any difference to our internal customers whether service is being provided by the facility staff or by that of a vendor – it should be transparent to the end user. In order for this to occur, the facility organization must treat the vendor as a customer. Some external service providers, such as food services, have special facility needs and may come to a stop if a facility element fails. They are special customers and require special attention.

8. *External tenants of buildings*

Many of you provide tenant/landlord services to companies or components of companies leasing space within your buildings. Your tenants are customers of the facility organization and should be identified as such.

9. The facilities themselves

Absolutely the most interesting response we have heard when compiling a list of our customers is "the facilities themselves." The concept didn't quite sink in the first time we heard it, but the more we thought about it, the more we agreed that the facilities were, in fact, your customers. Sometimes the facilities speak up and tell you that they are your customers when something goes wrong or needs to be repaired, but most of the time the facilities depend on you to be proactive and represent them. That is why you have preventive maintenance programs, conduct life cycle costing analysis and develop strategic master plans. You have a fiduciary responsibility to protect your buildings and you should think of them as customers.

How well did your management staff do? After you have developed a collective list of your customers, ask your management team to do the same exercise with their own staff. You want each and every individual within your organization to have a consistent answer to the question, "Who is your customer?'

SENSITIVITY TO CUSTOMER PERCEPTION AND EXPECTATION

Assuming that you become fully knowledgeable about who your customers are, you have yet another customer concept to incorporate into your old-fashioned service equation in order to help you better define service needs. Stop to consider the fact that customers have certain expectations about FM services as well as perceptions about the way the FM organization can deliver them. The combination of their predetermined expectations and their perception of you as a service provider, governs their assessment of the quality of your performance.

When there is no match between their expectation and their perception, you have a service gap. If their

A measure of quality for the customer is how close we come to their expectations about service and their perception of the way we perform.

expectations are higher than their perception of your ability to deliver, you have a *negative* gap. If, on the other hand, the perception matches the expectation, you have satisfied customers. Your customers have certain expectations and they perceive that you have the ability to live up to those expectations. It doesn't matter whether that perception is reality or fact-based because your customers use the perception factor as a benchmark of your service delivery capability. In test after test, when customers of facility organizations are polled about service, the results demonstrate that their evaluation of service delivery is based on both their *perception* and their *expectation* about service. You need to be able to understand your customers' expectations as well as their perceptions, in order to avoid gaps and have a positive match. For you to be able to narrow the negative gap between the customers' expectations and what the customers perceive to be the truth about your services, you must first understand what forms the basis of their expectations and perceptions. Knowing that you will be judged by both your customers' expectations and perceptions, it behooves you to 1) understand and 2) be able to measure them.

We must avoid a negative gap between expectation and perception.

We'll start with customer expectations. There are at least four factors which contribute to your customers' expectations, factors that provide you with sufficient information to be able to control, influence or manage their expectations. Let's see how customers develop expectations about service.

EXPECTATIONS ABOUT SERVICE

Customers bring a whole set of expectations about service with them to work each day. It is part of what experts call the "psychological contract"[2] related to the work environment. While it is not a written contract, your customers have a basic value system against which they judge how well the facility organization and the people within that organization perform. They start evaluating your services using the following criteria:

Do you know what a psychological contract is?

FIGURE 1.2

CUSTOMER EXPECTATIONS

Expectation Criteria	*Value*
1. The purpose of the service	Do they have a full understanding of the purpose of the service you provide? If they do not know the purpose, they cannot make a value judgment.
2. The degree of necessity	In the course of doing business with the FM organization, customers make a determination of how necessary the service is to doing business. If they perceive that your service is necessary to help them perform their jobs, they will have a high expectation level.
3. The degree of importance	There may not be a direct correlation between necessity and importance. It may not be absolutely necessary for them to have your service in order for them to perform their jobs, but they may perceive it as important to their jobs. If they think your service is important, they will have a high expectation level.
4. Their view of results	Individuals have their own perception of what constitutes results. They may have one view of outcome from your service which is entirely different from the truth. How they view this outcome drives their expectation about the way you provide the service.
5. The relative costs	The perception of costs is relative to each and every customer perspective. Some may consider the cost of your service to be extremely low if they value quick turnaround time, friendly service, customized service, etc. Others may be strictly bottom-line oriented and consider your service cost to be too high if they are disinterested in your approach.
6. The risks involved	Your customers will evaluate your service based on a risk factor. If they perceive any risk associated with doing business with you, their perception of the value-added benefit will be low. If, on the other hand, they feel that without your services they would be at risk, their perception of your value, and in turn their expectations about your service, will be extremely high.

Because your customers have a frame of reference from their lives outside the company, as well as an institutional memory from spending time within the company, they take the above criteria and add to them:

The anticipation factor. What heightens a customer's expectation level is anticipation about the service. They want a service to turn out a certain way. In some cases you actually add to that anticipation with visions of the "Office of the Future," and ergonomic and environmental claims that you are hard-pressed to deliver.

Customers bring a whole set of "baggage" with them about FM from the world outside their work life.

If you are designing a new space for one of your customer organizations, the individuals in the organization anticipate the way the space will look when it is finished. As the date for completion draws closer, their anticipation level gets higher and higher and their expectation about the service outcome may change dramatically. They visualize the space one way, while the actual space may be quite different. You also need to understand that most individuals cannot truly visualize new space from a two-dimensional drawing. If that is all you are using to demonstrate what their space will look like, don't be surprised if they are thoroughly confused about the way the space actually turns out. This gap between how they anticipate the space to be and how it actually turns out, is what drives their evaluation of your performance.

How many people do you know who can visualize new space from a drawing?

Previous experience factor. We don't know how many times we have heard customers say, "When so and so was in the facility organization, they did it this way and this is what happened." They either have had good or bad previous experiences with your organization and these experiences factor into the way they perceive your current performance. If all their experiences were good, they will expect their current experience to be so, but if the reverse is true, you will be starting with a negative expectation level. This is one reason why it is so important to know about the "I'm sorry concept" that we talk about later on in this chapter.

Customers have long memories when it comes to FM service. It's a known fact customers remember (and broadcast widely) negative perceptions about service rather than positive.

Comparison factor. Everyone makes comparisons about service. Our customers all have spouses, friends and colleagues who work in other companies and talk about the facility services there. Our customers themselves may have worked in other companies and have a basis for comparison. Or, because everyone thinks the provision of facility services is so easy, they may use their landlord or experiences from managing their own home and/or properties as a comparison basis. When they make these comparisons, they are not using a level playing field. They are not evaluating our services in the purest sense, but rather comparing them to some other external standard. You need to know what that standard is.

Third party information. This information is the most dangerous. Statistics say that dissatisfied customers have a tendency to tell at least eleven other people how unhappy they were with a particular service, and only two or three people when they are pleased. This means that bad news travels fast. We have never heard such a well developed hotline or information network as we have in the facility business. For example, all you have to do is tell customers they are going to move, and the war stories about how the facility organization handled someone else's move come out of the woodwork. No one ever talks about what a great job you did; they always mention that one box out of two million got lost, or that the ringer on the telephone in their new supply closet wasn't turned on. People love to share their misery with one another no matter how small it is, and this third party information has a strong impact on customer expectation about service.

The rumor mill plays havoc with customers and FM services. Misery loves company.

CUSTOMER PERCEPTIONS

Next, you must understand where your customers are coming from with respect to their perception of your ability to "deliver the goods." There is no magic formula for assessing customer perception, other than asking pointed questions to elicit information about it. If you don't believe this is important in your own company, give the following quiz to a random group of customers.

Don't be afraid to ask your customers how they perceive your services.

Ask them to complete the following statements, without any prompting from you. You will be amazed at the wide range of perceptions about service you encounter.

FIGURE 1.3

CUSTOMER PERCEPTION

1. The only way to obtain a parking space is to _____

   _____

   _____

2. The only way to get my space reconfigured is to _____

   _____

   _____

3. The only way to get a chair repaired is to _____

   _____

   _____

4. The only way to get the heating and air conditioning fixed is to _____

   _____

   _____

5. The only way to get satisfactory cleaning is to _____

   _____

   _____

6. The only way to (use your own example) is to _____

   _____

   _____

Your goal is to have a firm grasp of what your customers perceive your ability to be and make certain that it matches their expectations.

Just a short pause here to stress our point. You must always have human customer contact at every level of your organization from the technician to the facility manager. Whenever you are talking, briefing or just "schmoozing" with your customers, inquire about expectations and perceptions.

Using Expectation and Perception in Defining Customer Needs

Once you begin to have feedback from your customers on both perception and expectations, we think you will begin to see their value in assessing the quality of your facility services. Knowing what you now know about customer expectation and perception, you can incorporate this information as you define the needs of your customers.

We can put this information to good use. Move away from the traditional perspective of needs assessment.

The traditional needs assessment approach calls for you to identify the quantifiable needs of your customers, i.e., how much systems furniture they need, what kind of relocation assistance they need, or what type of telecommunications they need for employees who are telecommuting. If you expand your needs assessment approach to include their needs in terms of the value system or expectations we described above, you can create a service delivery framework which you can manage.

It becomes easier to provide FM services which are perceived by the customer to be timely, appropriate and of quality, if you understand what forms the basis of their expectations about your services from the start. We believe that a thorough understanding of your customers' perceptions provides you with the ability to use the information as a quality management tool to ensure that there is no perception gap. We see the match between expectation and perception as the baseline for having a satisfied customer.

To prove our point, let's turn to an authoritative source you know. You probably have read at least one of Tom Peters' books. In 1988, his book *Thriving on Chaos*[3] became an instant manual for modern managers on how to survive and be successful. In the book, he describes one of his basic tenets for dealing with customer expectations in terms of a service provider's ability to "under-promise and over-deliver." To his way of thinking, it is important to make certain that you manage your customers' expectations and their perception of your performance. Make certain that you never fail to meet your customers' expectations by promising them more than you can deliver.

Although it is no longer 1988 and today's business climate has changed, we feel that this advice still is very sound. We agree with Peters that one of the cardinal sins of customer service is to over-promise and under-deliver. This does more to create a negative gap between perception and expectation than anything else you can do to your customers. We do not want you to misconstrue our throughts, however, by so under-promising that you appear either incompetent or the perpetual negativist. It is a balancing act like most FM activities.

Never tell your customers you will do something for them and fail to deliver.

Meeting and managing your customers' expectations and perception about the way you perform becomes a baseline for FM. Having a satisfied customer becomes the common denominator in our business. Going beyond this baseline of service, however, is what Tom Peters and your authors think is the real measure of quality service. In other words, to satisfy a customer in today's environment is no longer good enough. You need to surprise your customers by exceeding their expectations and perceptions.

To reinforce what we and Peters have said, (and convince you that we know what we are talking about!), we turn to the "Kano model" for quality [4]. The Kano model, named for its creator, a Japanese quality management expert, differentiates quality in terms of the features of a service or product that a customer expects and the features a customer does not expect but is "delighted" to find.

Satisfying a customer is no longer enough. FM customers should be delighted!

"Ah ha!," you say. "They do know what they are talking about." "We have heard about delighting customers." Well, it comes from the Kano model, which confirms our notion that you need to go beyond the match between expectation and perceptions. According to the Kano model, traditional customer interaction (both in terms of needs assessment and marketing) has failed to achieve true quality because it has focused only on expected features of products and services and neglected the opportunity to go beyond the baseline to surprise and/or delight the customer. Remember the Kano model for quality, which says that:

A Delighted Customer Is One Whose Expectations
and
Perceptions Are Exceeded

Once again you are reeling from an overdose of theory by Cotts and Friday, but it was necessary to make the connection between expectations and perceptions, as well as the distinction between satisfying and delighting a customer. For those of you who are anxious to put theory into practice, we have translated all of the above for you into a working model to use with your customers.

Take a random group of FM customers and ask them to complete the following questions about a specific FM service *you have already provided*: In our example we have used space planning.

Do your own customer assessment.

FIGURE 1.4
_____

ASSESSING CUSTOMER DELIGHT WITH: *SPACE PLANNING*

1. My perception of the way the FM organization conducts space planning prior to my most recent project was:

   a. _____

   b. _____

   c. _____

   d. _____

   e. _____

2. My expectations for space planning by any FM organization include:

   a. _____

b. _____

c. _____

d. _____

e. _____

3. I was surprised and pleased when the FM organization performed/provided the following during my most recent space planning project:

a. _____

b. _____

c. _____

d. _____

e. _____

You have just assessed your customers' expectations about space planning services in general, their perception about the way your organization would provide these services (prior to involvement) and whether or not the things you did (or did not do) delighted your customer. Next you need to review your findings and interpret the data.

Gap when: expectation > perception.

First, you want to see if there is a gap between perception and expectation. If the answers to question 1 are negative, and do not match the answers to question 2, you have a service perception gap to begin with. Your customers' expectations are greater than their perception of your ability to deliver. If the answers to question 1 are positive and match the answers to questions 2, perception equals expectation. You have a satisfied customer.

Second, you need to see where you are on the delighted customer side. When the answers to questions 1 and 2 are positive and match, and there are positive answers to question 3, you have a very delighted customer. They have a positive perception of the way you will deliver services, but you also surprised them by doing more than they expected.

Satisfaction when: perception = expectation

Delight when:

perception = expectation

and you surprise your

customers by going above

and beyond! KANO!

You are in trouble here.

We are in the service

business where customers

are part of the process.

FM customers always

can't be right because...

You will have hit the jackpot if the answers to question 1 **exceed** the answers to question 2 **and** there are positive answers to question 3. They have certain expectations and their perception is that you will better those expectations. Even with all that, you still surprised them. Wow! In all honesty, this does not happen very often. Unless you already are doing a superior job of assessing their expectations or, due to some of the reasons we previously discussed they have relatively low expectations, customers typically will not have greater perceptions than expectations.

The FM organization really is in trouble if there are negative responses to question 1, and either nothing under question 3 or negative responses. It means that your organization doesn't come close to meeting expectations and customers have a serious perception problem with the way you perform. For those of you who uncover this problem, you have a lot of work to do. For starters, BUY FIVE MORE COPIES OF THIS BOOK, DISTRIBUTE THEM TO YOUR STAFF AND GIVE THEM A POP QUIZ EVERY WEEK UNTIL THEY GET IT RIGHT! Most of all, don't get upset and/or defensive. You may be doing everything right technically, but your customers' perception is what counts. Cooly analyze what you need to do to correct the perception problem and do it.

Is the Customer Always Right?

No discussion about quality FM service based on the premise that the customer drives the process would be complete without some attention paid to the debate over the issue, is the customer always right? From our perspective, we can't figure out why the issue should be up for debate in the first place. To our way of thinking, in the FM business, there is only one answer. Of course the customer isn't always right, and we'll tell you why.

First, you are in the FM *service* business, which is very different from selling widgets or hard goods. The customer can't always be right for any number of different reasons; he may have insufficient information, she may not know how to access your services, or he may not understand how the system works. There is a litany of reasons why the customer can't be right. You also are not in the retail business where the object is to have customers spend more money on hard goods. In the retail business, if the customer thinks he/she has gotten away with something, e.g. returning something that wasn't bought there, or getting a lower price than the ticketed one, that customer's tendency is to spend more money within the store. It doesn't matter if the customer purchased the item in the store or even if the store sells the merchandise, the establishment will go to great lengths to allow the customer to perceive (see, that word keeps cropping up) that he/she is right. This concept is not relevant to the FM business.

More importantly, however, we have an intrinsic problem with the customer-is-always-right idea, a problem which goes against the very fiber of what we are striving to promote with respect to quality FM. The customer is always right assumes that someone has to be wrong and that there is blame. If the customer is right, then the FM organization is at fault; or if the FM organization is right, then the customer is to blame. This passing of accusations may even pit FM organization components against each other, while the customer suffers in the middle. If you devote your energies to trying to figure out who is right and who is wrong, i.e., if you go through the classic finger-pointing routine, you never get to identifying your customers' expectations, sorting out their perception of how you perform your jobs and solving their problem. You will spend all your time in the "FM-Cover Yourself" mode and never become proactive with your customers. Let us relate what we have said above to a true-life FM story (this is not a fable).

Avoid trying to figure out who is right and who is wrong.

> There are two FM-related organizations within a Department of Administration. One FM organization provides design and engineering services and the other

Does this ring true?

performs operations and maintenance work. The two organizations rarely talk to one another (a separate problem for a separate chapter), so there isn't much coordination of effort. Enter the customer who has a problem. In a multi-million dollar laboratory filled with GC mass-spectrometer equipment, there are window leaks. The customer, worried about expensive equipment, calls the operations and maintenance group for assistance with the leak. After close inspection, they determine that the problem really isn't with the window, but rather with the slope of the roof, which causes the water to run down the side of the building rather than through the gutters. This group tells the customer that it isn't a problem for operations and maintenance, but one for design and engineering. In comes design and engineering and after careful study of the problem, this group determines that it isn't their problem either. The slope of the roof is correct, but operations and maintenance hasn't properly maintained the gutters so the customer was right in asking for assistance from operations and maintenance. The next thing you know, both groups are arguing with each other about whether or not the leak even exists! Is there any proof that the customer has seen a leak? And so it goes, on and on and on. In the meantime, the poor customer has pails under every window and waits for the demise of expensive equipment. So much for meeting or exceeding expectations. What do you suppose the customer's perception of the FM organization is now? Who is right and who is wrong? The bottom line is who cares? All the customer knows is that there is a problem and no one is solving it.

Right or wrong, the customer always is the customer!

So you need not worry about whether or not the customer is always right. What you should be worrying about is the fact that the customer will be there long after you have argued about right and wrong. Figuring out who is right and who is wrong doesn't change the basic fact that THE CUSTOMER ALWAYS IS THE CUSTOMER. It is plain and simple. You can't make the customer go away! Well, you can, but that isn't a subject with a pleasant ending for FM. Accept your customers for what they are and concentrate on things you can impact positively.

To test your skills on handling customers who want to start a dialogue about who is right or wrong, review the situation described below and determine how you would respond.

FIGURE 1.5.

UP ON THE ROOF

You are a relatively new facility director for the PDQ Company. You have been in your position for two months. You have just received a call from the Public Information staff director. He and his staff are located in the corporate tower building which is a leased facility. The building has 25 floors and the Public Information Office is on the 25th floor. The following is the Public Information Director's half of the conversation between the two of you.

"I understand that one of your staff told one of my staff that we cannot use the roof which we have used for the past five years at lunch time to get some sun." "Who do you think you are telling us that we cannot have a key to the roof?" "We have always used the roof for this purpose." "Your predecessor never told us anything like that and we are not going to stand for this." "Obviously you don't know who I am." " I will go to the CFO on this issue and get you fired if I have to." "We have been running this place for a lot longer than you have and you will do what we tell you to." "Remember, I am right about this. Do I make myself clear?"

DO WE NEED TO SAY "WE'RE SORRY"?

The FM business is ripe for understanding and implementing service recovery. As an example, if you execute 250 projects and 40,000 service orders annually, you are bound to make a mistake. For the most part these errors tend to be more errors of omission rather than commission. Stated very simply, service recovery is the ability to admit that something went wrong and recover from the mistake in a way that makes the customer feel you are truly sorry and want to correct the problem. In other words, the ability to say, "you're sorry" and then turn the situation around.

Sound familiar?

"Please forgive me."

The FM business is like live theater. We don't have the luxury of a second chance.

Nobody said we were perfect.

An article on service recovery which appeared in the July-August 1990 issue of *Harvard Business Review* made such a dramatic impact on one of your authors that it has since become the basis for a module in a customer service training course and is a huge success with FM organizations. The article hit home the point that service recovery does have a place in FM by this one statement: "The fact is, in services, often performed in the customer's presence, errors are inevitable."[5] You in FM provide a good number of your services in what we term "real time;" the customer is actually present, while you are performing the service. The customer is there to witness whether or not you perform correctly. When the customer is actively involved in or observing an FM service in progress, like the installation of a telephone or the issuance of a security badge, things happen. It doesn't matter that you have the best data on your customers, the best understanding of their need, the best technical staff and the best quality management program in place, in "live FM," sometimes you goof.

You all should have just uttered a huge sign of relief. Up until now you might have thought that throughout this book we were going to tell you that the only way to have quality FM was to be perfect all the time. How utterly ridiculous. The FM world is far from perfect and, having been practitioners in that world, we would never counsel our colleagues to pretend otherwise. While mistakes are inevitable, dissatisfied customers are not. While you cannot always prevent problems, you must learn to recover from them.

Mind you, we are not talking about FM *disasters*, like a roof blowing off during a hurricane or a flood of Noah's Ark proportions which wipes out entire buildings, but service situations which are recoverable. Our research with customers of FM services, as well as research on the service industry in general, shows that people are much more forgiving about the major service glitches than they are about broken promises on deliveries of systems furniture, late mail, or building hot and cold spots. Our customers want you to say you are sorry these things happen and then make amends. You need to accept this up front and then look for ways to turn a bad situation into a a good one. Let us give you a somewhat unusual, though real, FM example to illustrate our point.

> *The CEO of a small company was hosting a dinner for a delegation of visiting dignitaries from Japan on the night that the FM department had scheduled some major construction in another part of the building. The CEO planned a small dinner in the executive dining room followed by a presentation with overheads. The FM director had coordinated the construction with the CEO's office and everyone agreed there should be no problems which would interfere with the dinner. As an insurance policy, however, the FM director stayed in the building for the construction and gave the CEO his beeper number in case he needed anything during the evening or in the event of an emergency. True to form, things did not go smoothly and during the course of the work, just as the delegation was to sit down for dinner, the lights in the CEO's dining room went out. (Remember, this is a small company so there was no emergency back-up service). With not too much panic the CEO beeped the FM director, who immediately knew what had happened. Being a service recovery-trained (and brilliant!) FM manager, the quick thinking director called the dining room, explained what had happened, apologized to the group and asked them to give him ten minutes. Fortunately, there were two candle holders with candles on the table. He than ran to the construction department, grabbed hard hats with lights on them, sawhorses with yellow flashing lights and a large spot light and raced back to the dining room. Announcing that it would take 20 minutes to restore power, he outfitted each guest with a hat and placed the lights and sawhorses around the room. The Japanese guests gave him a round of applause. They had a ball and still talk about the unusual American dinner today. The CEO was praised for quick thinking under pressure, landed a contract with the visitors and gave the FM director a special award.* How's that for service recovery?

Learn to recover from a bad situation

Here is yet another real world FM example of service recovery.

> *One of your authors' FM organizations accepted a chair from a customer (and fellow colleague) for reupholstery. It was the customer's favorite chair and he was so attached to it he wouldn't even consider one that was more ergonomically designed. Unfortunately, while the chair was in the FM organization, it somehow got mixed in with other chairs destined for disposal. Tracking the chair after it disappeared involved an unbelievable sequence of good intentions going bad. Recovery from this incident was a personal embarrassment and required an eyeball-to-eyeball meeting and heartfelt apology, and an offer of a "chair menu" from which the customer could choose his next "seat of authority."* Service recovery can be hard!

Service recovery also gets kudos for the FM organization when a *customer* goofs, but you bail him/her out anyway. As we have said, the *customer* always drives the quality process, regardless of whether the customer is the one messing up. Suppose an organization moves from one space to another but forgets to notify the telecommunications group (which does not work for you) that they are moving and that their computers and the network must be relocated. Because your organization is so on top of things and knows how often this happens, you automatically take care of coordinating the de-install and re-install of computer equipment for the customer and end up as a hero. Not only have you *anticipated* the needs of your customers (as we discuss in Chapter Four), but you have *recovered* for them.

We will talk more about the way to make service recovery work in Chapter Five where we discuss training, but we need to say here that service recovery works best when all your FM staff is empowered with the ability to make decisions on the spot. In fact, we'll even go so far as to say that you won't have acceptable service recovery without empowered staff. One of the biggest complaints we hear from FM customers when we do focus groups for FM organizations is that the front line

Sometimes we have to cover for our customers' goofs!

person is powerless to make a decision and always responds with, "I'll have to go back and ask my supervisor." You can change that by understanding that FM managers usually are afraid that FM staff, if left to their own decision making, will give away the store and make the wrong decision. On the contrary, it is the FM managers who do this. Staff are much more cautious about spending FM dollars and usually make much more conservative decisions than their superiors. As we will talk about in Chapter Five, build some entrepreneurial capability into your FM staff by giving them certain parameters within which they have the power to make service recovery decisions. If a repair person is in someone's office to replace a broken troffer and accidentally breaks a picture of the family, let that staff member be the one to decide how to recover the situation and leave the customer with a positive feeling.

Empower the FM staff to make on-the-spot decisions. They need latitude and flexibility.

As a way of stimulating you and your staff's ability to recover from certain FM situations, we have developed some easy scenarios for you to discuss and come up with recovery solutions. After you have reviewed and discussed these, identify some actual situations from your own experiences and have your staff act out what they consider to be an appropriate recovery.

Test your skills.

FIGURE 1.6.

SERVICE RECOVERY SITUATIONS

1. Your headquarters building takes a long time to come up to temperature in the morning when it is cold and you typically start your heating system up late Sunday evening so it is warm by the time people arrive on Monday morning. After one particularly frigid weekend, you arrive on Monday morning to find that the building temperature is only 50 degrees. What do you do?

_____

_____

_____

2. You are moving a department of 200 people from one building across town to another building. You and your staff have planned every aspect of the move down to the last detail and have scheduled the move for an entire weekend. The timing is tight, but you know it can be done. On the first morning of the move you arrive at the building to wait for the movers. Two hours after the vans are slated to be at the building, the moving company calls to say that the two biggest vans have been in an accident on the beltway and it will be another two hours before new vans can be diverted to your building. You know that the tight weekend schedule will no longer work. It is your job to tell the department head that it will not be business as usual on Monday morning. How do you handle it?

_____

_____

_____

_____

3. You run a secure building and are in charge of the mail room which accepts and distributes all incoming mail including Federal Express, courier deliveries, etc. A scientist in one department calls the FM department early in the morning to say that she is expecting an important Federal Express package and needs to have it delivered as soon as it arrives. It is now 12:00 noon and your secretary sticks her head in the door to tell you that there is a "mad scientist" on the phone who didn't get her package. To make a long story short, when you check on the situation you find that the package is sitting on someone's desk and the person has gone to lunch. This is a two-part question. First, what do you tell the scientist and second, what do you do about the person who went to lunch?

_____

_____

_____

_____

Returning to the Customer...

In Chapter One we have devoted much of our discussion to defining and understanding customers. We think by now you will appreciate how important that concept is to quality FM. Before we leave this chapter and move on to other quality topics, we have a few summary points to make.

As we have said throughout our discussion, ascertaining customer needs sounds simple, but is, in fact, extremely complex, and the methods you use must always be reviewed to ensure that they are in step with your customers at any given point in time. First, we want you to remember that the burden for this activity, understanding and ascertaining customer needs, rests with you. You are the one who wants and needs to know the information and it is up to you and your staff to figure out how to obtain it. As a second consideration, you need to remember that no one technique works all the time for all categories of customers. What works with your top management may not work for tenants in your buildings. Thirdly, if you base your needs assessment solely on the written work or "number crunching" you will not have the complete story. Remember that you cannot learn about your customers by SIO. FM is a contact sport and that contact is with your customer. You must walk, talk and visit with your customers. Finally, make certain that you are drawing the right conclusions from your customer assessments by building in some good old-fashioned reality checks. Are you basing your needs on your understanding of the situation or on the expectations and perceptions of your customers? They are the drivers of the process and you need to make certain you are listening to where they want to go.

END NOTES

1. Spin doctor: an advisor or agent [esp. of a politician], who imparts a partisan analysis or slant to a story for the news media.

   Robert L. Chapman, *Dictionary of American Slang* (New York: Harper and Row, 1986), p. 408.

2. Psychological contract: tendency by an employee to assume that his organization has tacitly accepted the responsibility for enabling him to fulfill his unstated aspirations,

Saul W. Sellerman, *Management by Motivation* (New York: American Management Association, Inc., 1969), p. 51.

3. Tom Peters, *Thriving on Chaos* (New York, Harper & Row, 1988).

4. "Management Practices: U.S. Companies Improve Performance through Quality Efforts," *A Report to the Honorable Donald Ritter, House of Representatives* (Washington, DC: United States General Accounting Office, May 1991), p. 30.

5. Christopher W. L. Hart, James L. Heskett, and Earl W. Sasser, Jr., "The Profitable Art of Service Recovery," *Harvard Business Review*, July-August 1990, p. 148.

CHAPTER 2

TOTAL QUALITY MANAGEMENT (TQM) PRINCIPLES AND QUALITY FM

DECISIONS! DECISIONS!

We had a serious debate about where to place this chapter. On the one hand, the chapter is a summary of TQM principles and techniques. For many, it may even be an introduction to TQM. We've tried to strike a balance, to give you enough on TQM principles to help you in your FM practice, yet not bog you down with detailed mechanics. We hope this course of action meets with your approval!

THE APPLICABILITY OF TQM TO FM

We have heard from many of our colleagues that within both the public and private sectors the "bloom may be off the rose" with respect to formal TQM programs. Rather than formal TQM, our own experience and that of many of you suggest that "continuous process improvement" is the preferred approach to quality in FM. Regardless of what FM managers are calling their quality efforts, however, much of it has as its underpinnings the principles associated with TQM.

Quality FM has its underpinnings in TQM.

With that in mind, we debated long and hard about how to approach a discussion of TQM in our book. As we have said throughout Chapter One, our purpose in writing this book was to convince you that real quality within FM begins with the customer, and if your FM organizations understand and practice good customer service and marketing techniques, quality FM will be a natural outcome.

We would have been remiss, however, if we did not credit both the philosophy and principles of TQM with supporting our premise that the customer drives the process, as well as acknowledge the real contributions TQM has made to quality FM service. We also felt that there might be a few of you who were unclear about what TQM really is and undecided about its applicability to FM. In many ways it is not the "what" about TQM that is difficult for facility managers, but the "how" in terms of its implementation. This probably is where the real debate lies. We couldn't be more in agreement with basic TQM philosophy, but are finding that the implementation of TQM tools and techniques may be inappropriate or even a burden for most FM managers.

We decided it was our responsibility not only to include an overview of TQM, but also to incorporate actual FM experience with TQM and let you be the judge of what is right for your specific situation. We supposed that the best assistance we could offer was to help you make an informed decision about TQM. Above all, it is important for you to know that Total Quality Management is a long journey with few, if any, shortcuts and unlike other quality improvement efforts we will be discussing in subsequent chapters, TQM programs require tremendous commitment and involvement above and beyond the FM organization.

Both the philosophy and principles of TQM support our basic premise that the customer drives the process.

The difficult part for FM managers is the implementation part of TQM.

We want you to make an informed decision about TQM.

What Is This Thing Called TQM?

We probably spent more time on this section than any other in the book for the reason that so much has been written on quality that we didn't know where to start. As experienced facility managers, we also knew better than to reinvent the wheel, so we looked for existing source material to include in this discussion. To guide you through the maze of information on TQM, we prepared a three-part review of TQM consisting of a brief history on how it got started, a discussion on the recognized TQM "gurus" and how they differ, and the basic tenets of TQM philosophy. Your history lesson comes first.

TQM is a long journey with few, if any, shortcuts.

THE HISTORY OF TQM

In 1931 a statistician from Bell Labs, Walter A. Shewhart published unprecedented ideas on quality control. From his experience with manufacturing processes, Shewhart identified that all processes entailed variation which enabled him to define acceptable upper and lower limits for tasks. Through these limits Shewhart determined that one could detect variations and find their causes, which resulted in what he termed "statistical control." Workers on the floors of manufacturing plants could use these controls to plot and adjust variations. With this statistical base, quality could become a science and manufacturing could be monitored with measurable information which would allow future performance to be predicted.

Quality control started the TQM ball rolling.

Later, in 1942 when the Allied war cause was suffering, the idea of TQM first appeared. The advantage of acceptable quality levels was appealing for Army procurement officials who had to acquire large volumes of armaments from suppliers. With an unparalleled need for war materials, the War Department of the U.S. government established a Quality Control section which was staffed mostly by employees from the laboratories of Bell Telephone. One of Shewhart's disciples, W. Edwards Deming, taught statistical methods to those involved in the wartime procurement.

TQM came about during the war effort with the start of satistical control methods.

During the war effort, statistical control also proved to be a key element in acquiring military secrets, but by the end of the war, when the U.S. was enjoying newfound consumer prosperity, the interest in quality dwindled to the point where it was almost forgotten. [1]

Who Are the TQM Gurus?

One of our shared beliefs is that facility managers do not read professionally as much as they should, so we have tried to synthesize the work of those whom we consider to be the front-runners in the field of TQM. While the summary we have prepared is not intended to be exhaustive, we feel we have captured the essence of each thinker's philosophy with respect to quality.

It is important to know who the TQM experts are and how they got started.

Because of the way in which TQM started, many of the early works on quality were centered around the manufacturing environments which the early thinkers used as their quality laboratories. Until quite recently, most of the examples and case studies also came from the manufacturing milieu and it has only been within the past ten years that service industries were considered in the discussions about TQM.

Before our summary of the major points covered by those credited as being the quality management pioneers and "gurus" in North America, we felt we should provide a brief biography on each and the rationale for including them in our discussion. We do so with the hope that you will read, or at least scan, their works. These men have created a literal revolution in how many organizations function and you should be aware of their contributions.

W. Edwards Deming

When we first heard of TQM in the early 80's, both of us knew intuitively that there was much in TQM which fit perfectly with the way we felt facilities should best be managed. While we were writing this book, Dr. Deming died and we mark his passing by recognizing that so many of our colleagues have had his Fourteen Points on their walls since they first saw them. Since by education and practice he had a strong engineering bias, it was somewhat surprising to find he was the first quality consultant who used words like "leadership," "pride of workmanship," and "adopt a new philosophy." His influence on worldwide management is immense and he speaks directly to facility managers today.

Philip B. Crosby

Philip Crosby has been a major consultant in and proponent of improving work processes. Two of his concepts that have always resonated with us are his stress on the prevention of errors and his concept that hierarchical management is antithetical to good quality management. Crosby's work in this area obviously guides his personal life and vice versa.

J. M. Juran

J. M. Juran is another pioneer in quality management. His particular contribution was the concept of planning quality into goods and services. From a strong statistical base, he emphasized setting quality goals, planning quality into multifunctional processes and establishing quality planning databases.

Robert C. Camp

Robert Camp has written the Bible on benchmarking which compares an organization to others in a structured way so that one can learn from benchmarking partners. This technique is used to compare "best-in-class" or just another organization against which an organization wants to be measured. Camp stresses the importance of looking beyond pure metrics to identify the "why" of difference.

Karl Albrecht

Karl Albrecht, with his sometimes collaborator, Ron Zemke, applies quality management principles to the service industry. His particular orientation is on the customer and he emphasizes the importance of major attitudinal or paradigm changes by management and the need for attitudinal change throughout an organization.

Whether or not you plan on implementing a TQM program in your FM organization, we feel that some of the original thinkers in the area of quality are "must" reads. We hope we have you sufficiently titillated (that should wake you up!) by our review below, to seek out and read works by these experts yourself.

Figure 2.1

TQM Gurus and Their Subject Matter

W. Edwards Deming
- Fourteen Points for Management
- Need for a change of philosophy
- Cease dependence on inspection
- Emphasis on long-term relationships

- Continuous improvement
- Rigorous measurement
- Reinstate pride of workmanship
- Education and self-improvement
- Eliminate barriers between units
- There is one best way

J. M. Juran
- Quality planning
- Quality control
- How to improve quality
- Big Q and Little Q
- Measurement processes
- Quality goals

Karl Albrecht
- Quality in service
- The seven sins
- Uniqueness of service management

Philip B. Crosby
- Importance of prevention
- Principles of completeness
- The role of communication
- Elimination of managerial arrogance
- Systems integrity and measurement
- Identifying noncompliance
- Tying together your personal and professional life

Robert C. Camp
- Benchmarking
- Identifying comparative companies
- The performance gap
- Quantification strengths and weaknesses
- Benchmarking and business planning

- Understanding your customer
- Importance of training
- Making it permanent

Our list of TQM gurus is subjective. Read and learn from others.

Our list of TQM gurus is extremely subjective both in the names of the experts we chose to include and how we characterized their contributions. Perhaps you would have a different perspective on Juran or Albrecht or would include another guru whom you have found helpful. If so, you have zeroed in on one of our main points. Read and learn about TQM from others. The implementation of quality FM is a continuing journey and we all can learn from each other.

In that regard, we also want to offer a special tribute to Tom Peters and his various associates and coauthors over the years. Tom Peters is not a guru, as such, but his book *In Pursuit of Excellence* first chronicled the quality management revolution in industry in the United States and for many, he is one of the leading thinkers on quality management. He first introduced us to the growing quality movement in such a way that we could relate it to FM, but equally as important, we were "turned on" to his writing because he is so readable. His writing strikes a chord within us which resonates, "That's how we always believed in managing and providing services anyway." He remains today an enthusiastic and readable chronicler of American business management and service delivery.

A salute to Tom Peters.

WHAT ARE THE TQM PRINCIPLES?

Now that you are steeped in TQM history and know who we think some of the experts are, it is time to move ahead on the principles of TQM. As a first step, we felt it was only fair to provide a definition of TQM for you. You realize, however, that for every TQM expert, there is at least one definition of TQM. So we had a lot to choose from. Based on our hands-on TQM experience and working with organizations as consultants on TQM, we reverted back to the definition of TQM which made us feel most comfortable. We like the following as a definition of Total Quality Management.

> *A strategic, integrated management system for achieving customer satisfaction which involves all managers and employees and uses quantitative methods to continuously improve an organization's processes.*[2]

TQM defined.

With respect to the elements of TQM, we also felt it was unnecessary to try and rewrite what others have done so eloquently on the subject. Believe us when we say that there are far more knowledgeable authors on the subject of TQM than yours truly. Having conducted a fairly thorough literature search on the topic, we identified one article in particular which seemed to meet our needs. We feel an article written for the October 1993 issue of *Today's Facility Manager* by Alvin Elders, the Vice President of Quality at Haworth, Inc., provides one of the best descriptions of the principles of TQM from the perspective of FM we have seen. [3] We have taken excerpts from this article to highlight the six basic elements of TQM.

FIGURE 2.2

THE SIX ELEMENTS OF TOTAL QUALITY MANAGEMENT

1. Focus on the Customer

Where have you heard this before? As we stated in Chapter One, TQM dictates that you focus totally on the customer.

2. Continuous Improvement

A comprehensive TQM program is not just a one-shot review of processes. It is a continuous, dynamic and institutionalized system which can be used reliably over and over again. This element is proving to be the most enduring.

3. Process Management

The very core of continuous improvement is managing processes. In all types of work including FM, there are two types of processes. The first is processes which are apparent, like the direct management of a large construction project. The second process type includes those which are more ambiguous and creative, such as the interpretation of corporate strategies.

Management processes need to be assessed by four measurements: quality, delivery, cycle time and waste. There are standard methods in TQM (which we will review later) for reviewing processes to determine where they are redundant, complex, or ineffective. After processes have been streamlined and/or improved, they can continue to be assessed by these four criteria.

4. Management by Fact	W. Edward Deming was fond of saying, "In God we trust, all others must use data!"[4] and this is what he meant. In the TQM world, we need to have hard data to use as the basis for making decisions and we should be collecting this data on the four measurements described above.
5. Employee Involvement	One of the most critical elements of TQM is employee involvement. We take this basic TQM element and talk about employee *involvement* and *empowerment* in Chapter Five. Without employee involvement and empowerment a TQM program or, for that matter, any other quality effort, will not succeed. To maximize employee empowerment there must be a commitment to meaningful training.
6. Leadership	This is critical in a TQM program for not only does top management within the FM organization need to be committed to TQM, but it must be a commitment on the part of top management throughout the corporation. It is not enough for senior management to provide a framework within which TQM can thrive, but top management also must provide the leadership to allow change, improvement and staff empowerment to take place. TQM *requires new approaches to leadership, empowerment and groups on the part of top management.*

Source: From *Today's Facility Manager.* ©1993.

Because of his training and outlook, it always surprised us that Dr. Deming stressed the need for leadership. As a trained statistician, it always amazed us that in addition to his belief in data, he said, "Eliminate management by numbers and numerical goals. Substitute leadership."[5] It is the kind of statement one would expect from Tom Peters and serves as an indication of how progressive, for the times, Dr. Deming was in his early years.

Substitute leadership for management by numbers.

PONDERING THE PARADIGM SHIFT

Even if you know very little about TQM, you probably have heard about a requirement of TQM called "changing the paradigm." In the most simplistic of terms, a paradigm shift means changing a particular way in which we have been doing things. In other words, adjusting our role model for doing business. For TQM, the paradigm shift may mean a change in both organization behavior and service delivery.

Changing the way we do things.

For those of us in the FM business, there are three TQM paradigm changes which we feel are absolutely critical and we would characterize them as follows:

PARADIGM CHANGE ONE:

From	To
Giving customers what your organization thinks they need.	Giving customers what they tell your organization they need.

Or

The Customer Drives the Process.

Let customers tell you what they want.

Most of you are so good at the job of managing facilities that you think you always know what the customers want. FM organizations have a tendency to think they know how the customers want their space reconfigured, how the customers feel about a new building with inoperable windows, or why the customers want the office 10 degrees cooler *without ever asking the customers.* Because your organization has worked hard to develop models, policies, procedures and standards, you feel it must represent what is best for your customers. FM organizations have been so hard hit with the notion of service delivery readiness, they have a tendency to take the customers for granted and assume they know what the customers want all of the time. The paradigm shift requires FM organizations to forget about what *they* think the customers want and ask the *customers* what they really want.

PARADIGM CHANGE TWO:

From
Management assumes
that quality can be
achieved only by checks,
reviews, inspections,
controls and correction
of mistakes.

To
Management assumes that
quality begins with each
employee and that all
work is correct and at an
acceptable level of quality.
Services must be error-
free the first time.

Or

Do It Right the First Time

and

Empowerment to the Staff.

For FM, this paradigm change has an incredible impact on the way we do business because it means that
FM managers have to change their management philosophy. It means that facility managers must accept
the concept of empowering staff to perform according
to quality standards as defined by the customer and
must back away from the more traditional approach to
management which dictates a system of checks and
balances. This paradigm change also requires FM organizations to work on what it takes to provide FM services correctly the first time, which has a direct link to
paradigm change one. The only way to do it right the
first time is to make certain that you understand the
customers' needs up front before you provide the service. As we said in Chapter One, it means that FM
organizations have to focus on defining who the customers are and what their requirements are.

For the FM world as well, this paradigm shift means
that facility managers have to push decision making
down to the front line service workers who deal with
customers on a daily basis. These workers need to feel
not only that they are *able* to make these decisions, but
capable of making the right ones. For many facility
managers this concept is unnerving because they view
it as threatening their authority and power when, in
fact, empowerment really means sharing of power, not

Error-free service the first time.

Empowerment!

Change in management philosophy

Front line service workers need to be able to make decisions.

taking it away. For an untrained FM staff, however, empowerment can lead to organizational chaos. Your front line workers need both technical and customer service training. We will talk more about empowerment requirements in Chapter Five.

PARADIGM CHANGE THREE:

From	To
In order to change the status quo, improvement must be accomplished quickly and result in major breakthroughs.	In order to change the status quo, improvement must be incremental and occur over a long period of time. All breakthroughs are important.

Or

Commitment to Continuous Improvement.

Strive for gradual, results-oriented process improvement.

Our traditional approach to improvement, particularly process improvements, was tied to a belief that in order for change to have significant impact it had to happen quickly and result in monumental advancements. If, for example, FM organizations were going to change the way preventive maintenance was performed on equipment, a whole new set of policies and procedures was developed overnight and *voila*, a brand new way of doing business was put in place. The only problem with that approach is that the result was utter chaos. With a shift in the paradigm, gradual changes in the way of conducting preventive maintenance would mean the approach policies and procedures would be tweaked only slightly until they worked appropriately. The changes might not make a significant difference until all of them were implemented over a protracted time period. For those of you in the FM business who have been conditioned to fast turnaround times and quick response, the notion of gradual improvement should be a refreshing change. It does not alter the fact, however, that you must stay absolutely focused on results-oriented service delivery.

Is There A Difference Between TQM and a TQM Program?

We started this chapter by stating we had observed and heard from our colleagues in FM that there has been a decline in formal TQM programs. We know that the implementation requirements associated with formal TQM programs are labor intensive, time consuming and costly. For these reasons, many FM organizations have opted not to undertake formal TQM programs.

At the same time, however, we also have evidence that TQM *as a philosophy* is on the rise in FM organizations. Research conducted by IFMA (which we will discuss in a later section) and literature on TQM in FM prove that most FM organizations have either started or are interested in adopting TQM as a philosophy. Clearly the difference lies in the degree to which facility managers pursue a quality effort.

The difference lies in the degree of quality effort we pursue.

As facility managers, we hope after reading this book you will subscribe to a basic philosophy of quality defined by the customer. That is our first and foremost goal. It too is the number one element of TQM philosophy. We also believe in, and hope we are able to demonstrate in other chapters, the remaining five elements of TQM. We feel all six TQM elements constitute a successful recipe for success in providing quality FM service.

The six elements of TQM are the recipe for successful FM service.

By this time, your head is reeling from an overload of data (remember, we said data was important) on the topic of TQM and you probably are asking yourself if you really believe in quality, let alone a TQM program! Let us reassure you that most facility managers feel the same way after they have had a major dose of TQM. That is why we have devoted only one chapter to the topic. Before we go any further with our discussion on TQM versus TQM programs, we would like you to do a little self-assessment on how you feel *personally* about the concepts of TQM. This self-assessment will let you know if you as a facility manager are ready for any type of quality effort before you even consider a TQM program.

Figure 2.3

Where Do I Stand on TQM Philosophy?

Answer yes or no to the following questions. Remember, this is a self-assessment and you should be honest with yourself!

1. I believe the customer drives a quality FM service delivery system. _____ yes _____ no

2. I use data regularly in my decision making process and require the FM staff to do the same. _____ yes _____ no

3. My management style encourages staff to take risks and make decisions. _____ yes _____ no

4. I want to develop an organization climate where staff feel empowered about their work. _____ yes _____ no

5. I have made a commitment to provide resources for staff training in areas other than technical FM, particularly customer service. _____ yes _____ no

6. I will make a commitment to provide the time for managers and staff to work on improving the quality of FM services. _____ yes _____ no

7. I agree that we have a need for process improvements in the FM organization. _____ yes _____ no

8. I believe that teams play a significant role in a quality-oriented FM organization. _____ yes _____ no

9. I am not afraid to be measured or have my organization measured. _____ yes _____ no

10. I believe that I provide leadership to the FM organization. _____ yes _____ no

11. I will ask my staff to take this self-assessment test. _____ yes _____ no

If you answered no to any of the questions, you need to rethink the idea of quality FM. In order for you and your organization to be successful at FM quality, you need to accept and be willing to invest in the six elements of TQM.

Where we differ with TQM is in the implementation of the philosophy. For us it is how you choose to bridge the gap between Total Quality Management and a Total Commitment to Customer Service. It may be easier for you to understand what we mean if we use a simple graphic to illustrate our point.

FIGURE 2.4

BRIDGING THE PHILOSOPHICAL GAP

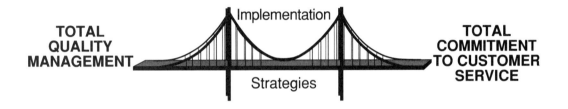

You may be saying that all this is well and good and you thoroughly understand the difference between TQM philosophy and a TQM program. What you may be asking at this stage is, "What constitutes a TQM program? Are there specific components?" To assist you in determining whether or not a formal TQM program makes sense for your FM organization, we have developed a list of the components of a TQM program as they are practiced in most companies and agencies.

Figure 2.5

Components of a Formal TQM Program

Component	Explanation
• Executive-level buy-in to TQM and a TQM program.	• Corporate buy-in to the commitment concepts of TQM and willingness to support a TQM program.
• TQM vision statement.	• TQM has to be incorporated into the corporate business vision.
• Establishment of a Quality Council or Executive Steering Committee.	• An oversight body needs to be established for a TQM program.
• Establishment of a TQM program management strategy.	• Top management needs to determine its strategy for a TQM program. What will the TQM program infrastructure look like?
• Establishment of an implementation schedule for TQM program.	• A schedule needs to be established for implementing TQM. Either all organization units will be "on-line" with TQM at the same time or pilot programs will be established and organizations phase in TQM programs.
• Conducting a training needs analysis.	• Organizations have to know what skills their employees have and what training they will need for TQM.
• Establishing TQM budget.	• Funding has been set aside for training, process improvements, staff down time, management reviews, etc., associated with TQM.
• Identifying and selecting TQM program suppliers.	• Often it takes more expertise with TQM programs than in-house management and staff have. Contractors for training and analysis may be required.
• Training staff in TQM and related subjects.	• Staff must be trained in the basic philosophy of TQM and in related skills areas such as problem-solving, teaming, leadership, etc.

- Developing standards and measures for TQM.

- Establishing process action teams and other teaming arrangements.

- Monitoring and measuring results.

- Establishing a system for recognizing and publicizing TQM results.

- Adjusting the TQM process based on results and suggested process improvements.
- Institutionalizing the TQM process.

- Significant time must be devoted to the way in which quality will be defined and how it will be measured.
- The use of teams is a major component of the empowerment philosophy.
- The outcome of TQM efforts must be monitored and measured.
- Feedback to teams, management and other organizations on TQM results is essential.
- The process is fluid to allow for change.
- In order for TQM to be effective, it must be institutionalized. It cannot be a one-time effort.

While this is not an exhaustive list of the components of a TQM program, it is comprehensive enough to make our point that a TQM program requires time, financial resources and commitment.

Before you embark on the long TQM journey, we recommend that you take the simple test we have provided below to determine if your FM organization and the company as a whole are ready for a Total Quality Management program.

A comprehensive TQM program requires staff time, financial resources and commitment.

FIGURE 2.6

IS A FORMAL TQM PROGRAM RIGHT FOR YOUR FM ORGANIZATION?

Answer yes or no to the questions listed below.

CORPORATE ISSUES

1. Has corporate management made a commitment to TQM? _____ yes _____ no

2. Has corporate management incorporated TQM into its mission statements? _____ yes _____ no

3. Are other organizations in the company implementing TQM?   _____yes   _____ no

4. Is the corporate culture supportive of change?   _____yes   _____ no

5. Has corporate management made a commitment to provide the necessary resources for TQM training?   _____yes   _____ no

6. Has corporate management made a commitment to establishing an organization infrastructure to manage and review TQM progress?   _____yes   _____ no

7. Has corporate management made a commitment to the time required away from service delivery to support a TQM program?   _____yes   _____ no

FM Organization Commitment

1. Are you knowledgeable about TQM program requirements and commitments?   _____yes   _____ no

2. Are you willing to provide your staff with TQM and related skills training costing between $700 and $10,000 per employee?   _____yes   _____ no

3. Is your organization able to make financial commitments to a long-term TQM effort?   _____yes   _____ no

4. Will you commit to TQM process reviews?   _____yes   _____ no

5. Will your organization be able to provide its customers with the same level of service while undergoing a TQM program?   _____yes   _____ no

6. Can you make a 3 to 5 year commitment to a TQM program?   _____yes   _____ no

If you answered no to any of the above questions, a comprehensive TQM program probably is not a good idea for your FM organization. As we said previously, it is not enough for you and the FM organization to be committed to a TQM program. Without the complete buy-in and support of corporate management, a comprehensive TQM program may not be the answer to your quality needs. It doesn't make sense for an FM organization to embark on the TQM journey if they will be met with opposition or lack of understanding from top management and the last thing facility managers need is to set themselves up for failure.

A TQM program requires complete buy-in and support of top management.

FM EXPERIENCE WITH TQM TO DATE

We told you earlier in the chapter that we would review what we know about FM experience with quality programs so far. As you continue on in the book, you will note that Chapter Six is dedicated to showcasing the "Best Practice" quality efforts of your colleagues. From an analytical standpoint, the most inclusive study on FM experience with quality and quality programs that we are aware of at the time we wrote this book was conducted by the Gallup Organization Inc. of Princeton, New Jersey for IFMA in 1992.[6] In 1992, Gallup contacted and interviewed 501 facility managers who were selected to participate in the study at random from a list provided by IFMA. The study focused on quality programs within FM organizations and only briefly explored quality issues from a corporate perspective. It is important to point out that the study did not specifically ask participants to discuss TQM programs exclusively, but quality programs in general. The findings we have summarized include information in the areas of:

FM organizations report on their TQM experiences.

- Quality activities;
- Effectiveness of quality programs; and
- Benefits of quality programs.

Quality Activities

The IFMA survey asked participants to comment on the quality activities their FM organizations used. Because the question was general with respect to quality, participants interpreted quality programs in different ways. About 75% of those questioned stated that their FM organization was involved in some type of quality effort and over 50% said their activities were targeted towards customer service improvements. Figure 2.7 depicts responses on quality program activity.

Figure 2.7

Quality Activities of FM Organizations

ACTIVITY	TOTAL (n=500)	INDUSTRY GROUP		
		SERVICE (n=294)	MANUFACTURING (n=161)	OTHER (n=45)
Group Interactive Activity (Team approach, Quality audit, Safety committee meetings and Problem-solving meetings)	24%	19%	31%	24%
Management Improvement/Programs (TQM and Mission of the company)	17%	14%	21%	22%
Customer Feedback/Input (Customer satisfaction survey)	15%	17%	8%	0%
Data Collection (Benchmarking, Internal/external tracking and Quicker response time)	9%	9%	10%	8%
Training (Crosby program and Deming process)	9%	9%	14%	9%
Improve Facilities/Equipment (Remodeling, Ergonomic furniture/lighting and Improving equipment)	9%	11%	4%	12%
Internal "Quality-Control" Programs (Cost control, Internal quality, In-house reduction, Quality assurance program and Error rate reduction)	9%	9%	10%	0%
Energy/Environment Programs (Recycling program, Air quality, Energy management and Environmental program)	7%	8%	5%	14%
Company-wide Program	6%	4%	8%	7%
Continuous Improvement Process	6%	4%	12%	2%
Recognition Programs (Malcolm Baldrige Award, Employee recognition and Awards program)	5%	5%	5%	4%
Employee Suggestion Program	2%	3%	0%	0%
Other Programs	6%	9%	4%	9%

Source: From Quality Programs in Facility Management, Research Report #9. ©1992 by IFMA.

EFFECTIVENESS OF QUALITY PROGRAMS

The study guide identified fifteen quality programs and asked participants to rate the effectiveness of the program on a one-to-ten scale with "10" being the highest rating and "1" being the lowest. Of the programs listed, problem-solving groups, work teams, employee training on quality techniques and employee involvement teams rated the highest and were considered to be the most effective. Quality councils, suggestion systems and statistical process control programs were rated the lowest. Figure 2.8 identifies the quality programs included in the study and their ratings with respect to effectiveness.

BENEFITS OF QUALITY PROGRAMS

Another component of the IFMA study was an analysis of the benefits FM organizations felt they derived from involvement with quality programs. According to the FM managers polled, the most significant benefits were obtained in two areas:

- *Service to FM organization customers*

  The study results indicated that quality efforts enhanced the reliability of services to internal customers, improved communications with others in the company, increased overall internal customer satisfaction and accelerated the delivery of service to internal customers.

- *Internal FM organization work processes*

  In addition, work procedures, work order processing, per-person productivity, department costs, and error and defect rates were somewhat positively impacted by quality efforts.

One aspect of the study which we feel is important to share with our readers is the result of the question on impact of quality programs on FM costs. Most participants reported a decrease in their organization's costs amounting to approximately 9%. Of the respondents, 39% reported that quality improvement efforts resulted in company savings or decreased expenses by more than 5%.

Advice: know what you are getting into with a TQM program, but don't be afraid of a quality improvement effort.

Figure 2.8

Effectiveness of Quality Programs

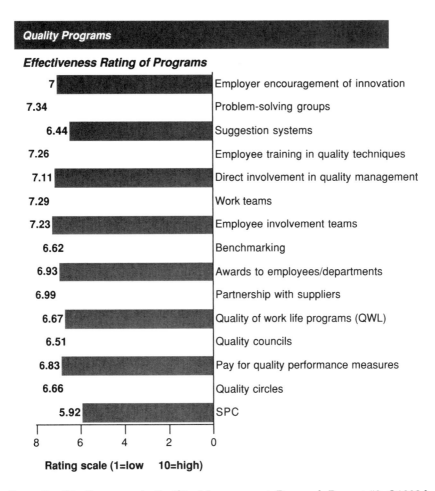

Effectiveness Rating of Programs

Rating	Program
7	Employer encouragement of innovation
7.34	Problem-solving groups
6.44	Suggestion systems
7.26	Employee training in quality techniques
7.11	Direct involvement in quality management
7.29	Work teams
7.23	Employee involvement teams
6.62	Benchmarking
6.93	Awards to employees/departments
6.99	Partnership with suppliers
6.67	Quality of work life programs (QWL)
6.51	Quality councils
6.83	Pay for quality performance measures
6.66	Quality circles
5.92	SPC

Rating scale (1=low   10=high)

Source: From Quality Programs in Facility Management, Research Report #9. ©1992 by IFMA.

Having reviewed quality programs, our best advice is "look before you leap" into a comprehensive quality program, but don't be afraid to start a quality improvement effort. Our second piece of advice is don't delay in getting started. Take as big a bite out of the "quality" apple as you can. Read as much as you can about quality management and talk to your colleagues. Network with them as they are a tremendous source of encouragement and inspiration and they will give you honest answers to your questions. They also know the pitfalls. Go to both commercial and professionally sponsored training on continuous improvement. Do all of these things, but DON'T PROCRASTINATE! Start today. Even though you think you may be over-committing yourself and your FM organization, err on the side of over-commit- ment. Partial success is better than the status quo.

As you will determine from subsequent chapters, most of what you will be doing is attitudinal. Don't overburden yourself or your staff with TQM mechan- ics; implement new techniques only when you have a psychological "buy-in," resources to implement and the means to sustain that technique for at least two to three years. We will show you that there are ways other than formal TQM programs to provide quality FM ser- vices and will provide some "Best Practices" on what others have done. In other words, just go do it!

END NOTES

1. "From Top Secret to Top Priority: The Story of TQM," *Aviation Week & Space Technology*, May 21, 1990, pp. S7- S24.

2. *Total Quality Management: An Overview, Student Manual*, General Services Administration, GSA Training Center, (Washington, DC, June 1990), p. 11

3. Alvin Elders. "QM for FMs: Can Total Quality Manage- ment Programs Make a Difference?," *Today's Facility Manager*, October, 1993, pp. 1 and 4-43.

4. Mary Walton, *The Deming Management Method* (New York, NY: The Putnam Publishing Company, 1986), p. 96.

5. W. Edwards Deming, *Out of the Crisis* (Cambridge, MA: Massachusetts Institute of Technology Center for Ad- vanced Engineering Study, 1986), p. 24.

6. *Quality Programs in Facility Management*, Research Re- port #9 (IFMA, 1992), pp. 2-7.

CHAPTER 3

MEASURING QUALITY AND CUSTOMER SATISFACTION WITH FACILITY SERVICES

ARE WE THERE YET? MEASURE! MEASURE! MEASURE!

You may remember in our introduction we talked about five pillars of quality, one of which was that you must be willing (and able) to measure and be measured. "Why," you might ask, "is measurement so critical?" Just think about this. How can you tell if you are improving continually if you do not measure? Measurement is so important that we are devoting an entire chapter to it. If for no other reason, common sense should tell you that the best way to be able to assess what you need to do to improve is to establish a baseline of where you are and then, through measurement, determine how you compare. But, common sense doesn't always prevail in the FM business.

Third Pillar of Quality: benchmarking and metrics are essential.

As you recall from Chapter Two, we mentioned measurement as one of the universal principles for the quality management of facilities and one of the six elements of TQM. If you look at the educational backgrounds of most of the early proponents of TQM, who were engineers in manufacturing environments, it is not surprising that measurement is an integral part of that movement. From our perspective, with respect to FM, we cannot even entertain the thought of you managing your organization without the use of measure-

To manage your organization you need measurement and statistical analysis. Establish a baseline of where you are.

ment and statistical analysis if you are going to be a success.

THE WILLINGNESS TO BE MEASURED

One of the characteristics we all admire in most athletes is that they are willing to be measured, daily during their season. We admire that willingness in facility managers too, and wish that it were a more prevalent characteristic of our compatriots. Since most of you really do a great job, why aren't you willing to document that?

It has been our experience that some facility managers are almost paranoid about measurement. In fact, we have known a manager of a major facility who was so afraid to measure and be measured that he actually hurt his image within his own organization AND DID IRREPARABLE DAMAGE TO HIS DEPARTMENT. His organization was top-flight in providing a high volume of responsive services and in satisfying customers to a high degree, but because of his paranoia, those great results were neither documented nor reported to management. Even when the results were gathered by his staff and shown to him, he declined to embrace or use them. What business do you think he is in today?

Don't be paranoid about measurement.

Your concern as a facility manager is that your measurement reflects reality.

While this may be an extreme case, we find it not atypical of many of your colleagues. Part of this is caused by a feeling than any down tick of a favorable trend is a blot on your management record, when what you really should be concerned about is that you are measuring the right things, in the right way, so that you really know what is going on within your organization. Regardless of your approach to quality management, analysis of data and measurement, both qualitative and quantitative, should be a major factor in your management decisions regarding FM service delivery. Your concern as an FM manager is that your measurement reflects reality so that you are getting the information, whether it is good or bad, which will allow you to make informed management decisions.

WHY ARE FACILITY MANAGERS UNWILLING TO MEASURE AND BE MEASURED? WE THINK IT IS FOR SEVERAL REASONS:

- *First*, FM managers have totally adulterated the concept of zero defects as a goal, vigorously to be pursued, never to be reached. Too many FM managers, in our experience, manage as if they never made a mistake, will never make a mistake, and, for sure, will *never* admit that they made a mistake. Yet, because you are human, you really make mistakes every day. Some of the manipulations that have gone on to cover up mistakes are the exact antithesis of quality management.

- *Secondly*, too few FM managers feel, given the scope of their duties, and the reactive nature of some of them, that they can stay on top of all aspects of their job to the degree that they are willing to keep detailed statistics measuring them. What you forget is that you will be judged primarily on trends. In other words, does the trend data show that your organization has made an attempt to improve. While your baseline may be low, what have you done to raise it? If you measure and improve, you can show management that you are headed in the right direction. If not, perhaps you are not suited for a facility *management* job. If you don't measure, then it is simply conjecture whether you have done a good job. For example, when the time comes to make a determination about where your organization is headed in the future — THE BIG "O" WORD (outsourcing) — you will not be able to defend your case.

  You will be judged on trend data.

  You need to defend your case.

- *Thirdly*, you have already heard us talk about how you need to get closer to your customers and when we are talking about measuring your customers' evaluations of your service, we are convinced that some facility managers are afraid of their customers. We believe part of the reason is that you hear so many complaints. It is tough to be in a job where customers only talk to you when something goes wrong. You need your customers, however, because they can make a difference when it comes time to defend your

  Some facility managers are afraid of their customers.

Unwillingness to be measured is a sign of insecurity.

position. If your customers think you are doing a good job and providing an essential service, they will be loyal and can help you with top management. The bottom line is don't underestimate your customers; you need them!

In summary, an unwillingness to talk about or proactively pursue being measured is a real sign of insecurity, and in today's business environment, this is not a healthy attitude. Instead of worrying about being measured, you should worry about designing a system that:

- Reflects reality (it measures what is really important about us);
- Captures the data correctly;
- Can be sustained and does not become so routine that it loses meaning; and
- Can be administered without an unreasonable diversion of resources to reporting and analyzing.

If you stay with us for the rest of this chapter, we will help you do this.

SO WHAT DO YOU USE, A RULER OR A SCALE?

Exactly how much measurement is enough and do you have to have a sophisticated measurement system or a simple, homegrown one? We think the important point about measurement is deciding up front what needs to be measured. You recall from Chapter Two that the TQM gurus talk about measuring:

Decide up front what needs to be measured.

- Quality;
- Delivery;
- Cycle time; and
- Waste.

We translate these into:

- How effective are you in providing services?;
- How efficient are you in providing services?;

- How responsive are you?; and
- How relevant are both your services and your ratings?

By *effectiveness* we mean do you get the job done and how well do you do it? It is perhaps the most common-sense-based of the measurements. But whose definition of effectiveness do you use? You, as the facility manager, might want effectiveness of your annual renovation program measured in terms of whether all space, engineering, and interiors standards were met. If they were, you might rate yourself at 100%. Your customers' criteria, however, might be how many extras they were able to talk you into or how many of their last minute changes you accommodated, resulting in a 50% rating.

Which is correct? Remember the expectation and perception discussion from Chapter One? If you agree with us that the customer drives the process, then the customers' criteria are the ones you need to use as your measures. At the same time your boss, as one of your customers, might judge your performance on effectiveness as you would, from a standards viewpoint. You may need to have an effectiveness measure which serves both the expectations of your organizational unit customers, and one which meets the expectations of top management.

Efficiency relates to how well you produce outputs in terms of resources. What we call cost-effectiveness is really a measure of efficiency. Most often we measure efficiency in terms of dollars/sq. ft. or sq. ft./person. Usually, it is efficiency factors that we use when we benchmark against similar or "best-in-class" organizations. While efficiency measurements tend to be the most purely mathematical, there may be other internal organizational, management, and reporting measures which constitute efficiency that are specific to your particular company or agency. For example, efficiency may be measured by how many moving service orders were filled in a month.

Use the customers' criteria as your measure.

If you don't define and share your standards, each customer will have a different perception.

Responsiveness is different from effectiveness in that it is more a measure of timeliness. From your customer's perspective, how many times did you complete your projects in a timely fashion? Responsiveness becomes one of the most controversial of measures with your customers, because the FM organization often has a different perception of timeliness than the customer. This is a classic example of "managing customer expectation." For example, if you don't share with your customers your standard that says it will take an hour to respond to hot and cold calls, your customer may expect you to be there in ten minutes. When it comes time to evaluate the responsiveness of the FM organization, you will receive poor marks.

By the same token, if you tell your customers that your standard for responding to hot and cold calls is ten minutes, but you do not tell them that your standard time for removing a wall from their office is two weeks, your customers might assume that it will take ten minutes as well. Again, their evaluation of your responsiveness will be low. Your customer's perception is that all FM services will be provided immediately after a request has been made, unless we educate them as to a standard for responsiveness.

You need to make certain that before you start measuring the responsiveness of service, you and your customers are operating from the same knowledge base. It is essential for FM organizations to share their standards for service delivery, if they want their evaluation of responsiveness to be positive. You might, for example, publish a service standards handbook, or a newsletter on service order requests or have standards in your service directory.

Customers assume basic FM services will be there. They tend to emphasize services that affect practice, comfort and personal effectiveness.

To dramatize the importance of responsiveness as a measure, we have developed a simple exercise (Figure 3.1) which you can use within your FM organization. Pick any service you provide to a customer and identify the completion standard you have established for that service. In the next column, write down how you communicate that standard to your customer. Finally, do a

FIGURE 3.1

FM Service Delivery Responsiveness

Service and Standard	Means of Communicating Standard to Customers	Customer Understanding of Standard
1.		
2.		
3.		
4.		
5.		
6.		
7.		
8.		
9.		
10.		

Have the FM organization complete columns one and two and a representative customer population complete column three.

---

quick check with one of your customer populations by asking them to identify what they think is the standard for each of the services you identified. If you find that 1) you have not created or published the standards, and 2) your customers have a different perception of what the standard is, you will not be pleased with a formal evaluation of your responsiveness measure.

Finally, you need to measure if your services are *relevant*. At first blush it sounds almost comical that you would even consider irrelevant services, but 1) some services are more important than others to a customer, and 2) when we are forced to cut back, who

Customers need to tell you if your service means anything to them.

determines what is irrelevant? Time and time again, when we work with customers of FM organizations and ask them to prioritize the services they think are relevant and then ask the FM organization to do the same, the list is different. As an example, an FM organization might state that their most relevant services are those that affect health, safety, security and company operations. Customers, on the other hand, often assume that those services will be there (until the rare time that they aren't) and tend to attach a greater relevance to an FM service which affects their own department or personal effectiveness, prestige or comfort.

The key is to perform the "right things right."

Sometimes your attitude as facility managers fails to accommodate the differences in the perception of relevance to an organization. As a fairly simple measure, you can look at ten services you provide to your customers and determine their relevancy. We recommend that you use the following format as a test to determine the differences in perception of service relevancy among you, your staff and your customers.

Figure 3.2

Relevancy of FM Service

Facility Mangers: List, in priority order, the ten services you provide which you think are the most relevant to your customers.

1. _____
2. _____
3. _____
4. _____
5. _____
6. _____
7. _____
8. _____
9. _____
10. _____

Facility Management Staff: List, in priority order, the ten services you provide which you think are the most relevant to your customers.

1. _____
2. _____
3. _____
4. _____
5. _____
6. _____
7. _____
8. _____
9. _____
10. _____

Sample Customer Population (choose any customer group): List, in priority order, the ten services provided by the FM organization which you think are the most relevant to your department.

1. _____
2. _____
3. _____
4. _____
5. _____
6. _____
7. _____
8. _____
9. _____
10. _____

Were you surprised by the differences? We probably demonstrated our point that relevance of FM service for you and your staff may not be the same as it is for your customers.

The quality facility manager has adequate analytical skills.

USING THE RIGHT METRICS OR I DON'T KNOW A P-CHART FROM A HISTOGRAM

One of our principal reasons for writing this book was to de-mystify the quality movement and allow facility managers to really understand how to apply the common-sense parts of quality management which may be overshadowed by more formal TQM. When it comes to the use of metrics, if you are around the TQM devotees or read the literature, it is easy to get confused about the measurement aspects because it appears as if they are applicable only for a Ph.D. in theoretical mathematics. We are here to tell you that it doesn't have to be that way.

Before we talk about measurement tools to use with your customers, we need to take a few minutes to talk about the measurement skills you need to know. Basically, you need to have five measurement skills to maximize what you, as an FM manager, can gain from our version of old-fashioned quality management.

1. You will want to do some trend analysis. For example, over the past six months, what have your project management costs looked liked for construction projects?

2. You will want to understand the normal distribution of data. For example, if you perform a large number of repetitive tasks well 85% of the time, is that good or bad?

3. You need to know a little bit about how to set up measurement instruments to increase their validity. For example, should you ask customers on a questionnaire whether they are satisfied with your services by answering "Yes" or "No" or should you give them a rating scale of 1 to 10?

4. You will want to be able to compare the performance of your department against like organizations or "best-in-class" organizations through benchmarking. For example, how do you compare with organization X when it comes to churn rates?

5. You will want to try and improve your processes by

controlling them through Statistical Process Control (SPC). For example, what are the upper and lower control limits for your process of responding to a chiller malfunction compared to the average?

We could hear the echoes of the shock waves reverberating in our ears as we wrote the above, and we suspect many of you think we have only added to your confusion. While these measurement skills still may be difficult to comprehend, we have provided more concrete examples of each which we hope will make the skills more real for you.

1. Using trends analysis (without being trendy!)

You use trend analysis all of the time in your business, although you may not recognize it. For example, as Figure 3.3 indicates, when you look at service orders accomplished for the first six months of the year and see they have averaged a 10% increase per month then, absent other pertinent information, you probably could conclude that the trend would continue for the second half of the year. You also would see that if the trend continues, in December, your service order work load would be 568 service orders and you had better staff up to meet that load. A closer analysis, however, reveals that the real increase in work orders occurred April through June and that increase averaged 20% per month. If we project that trend out, we can predict that the December workload will be 856 service orders, perhaps requiring quite a different staffing for our department.

FIGURE 3.3

TOTAL WORK ORDERS ACCOMPLISHED

Acme, Inc. Facility Department

January	February	March	April	May	June
200	210	200	200	280	320

Analysis + common sense
= success.

Actually, as an experienced facility manager, you are aware that certain events and times of the year generate peaks and valleys in service orders. By looking at experience data from other years, you can detect those trends. What you learn from looking at such trends is that few things in our business (workloads, expenses, user evaluations, etc.) can be projected by straight line extrapolation and that you would be better off projecting a band of possible results and accommodating to the results within that band. In our example, the six month projection shows a 10% per month increase of service orders while the last three months shows a 20% per month increase. If those differences require a change of staffing, you might try to hit the middle ground. Absent any knowledge of a historical peak or valley, you might plan that your workload increase will be about 12-16% per month in general terms. If you are aware of a peak or valley in service orders that historically occurs during May and June, then you would adjust the projected result by the amount that the peak or valley deviates from the norm.

This is one of the best examples of our adage to combine the analyses used in quality programs with the common sense of historical trend data and experience.

2. Using the normal distribution of data (Is my organization normal?)

Figure 3.4 may be a familiar sight to you, but you may not know that it is the normal distribution of a large volume of randomly occurring events. For the moment, just ignore what random means. A good rule of thumb is that unless you know differently, assume randomness. This means that your data will array itself in a familiar bell curve and you can draw several conclusions about that data.

First, using a calculator, you calculate the mean and the standard deviation of your data. About 68% of your data occur within one standard deviation of the mean, about 95% within two standard deviations, and 99.7% within three standard deviations.

Okay, stop screaming! "How, you ask, is this useful?" Imagine that you suspected that you had a light bulb problem (your bulbs seem to be burning out prematurely) and wanted to be 95% sure that you didn't? You could get the manufacturer's data on when the bulbs burned out and then analyze your own data. If your data fell over two standard deviations (or what is called 2 sigma) from the mean, you would have a right to complain to the manufacturer that, as a minimum, you did not have lights that met their specifications. While this might seem like a lot of work to go through for a light bulb, if you needed to address this type of problem with a manufacturer, you would have to perform this type of analysis because they certainly would have performed it in-house to come to their own defense.

FIGURE 3.4
___

NORMAL DISTRIBUTION OF DATA

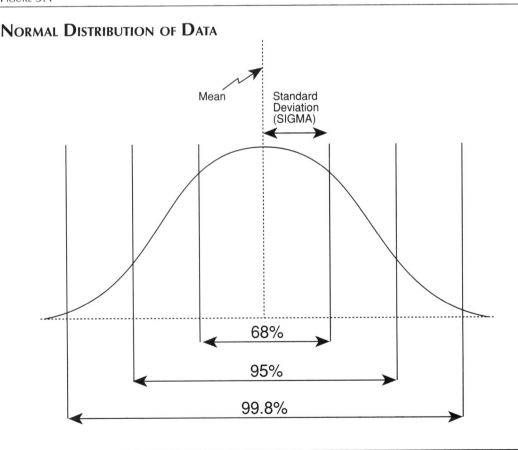

3. Using measurement instruments to increase their validity

While we are going to have a more detailed discussion about customer involvement in measurement in the next section, we have included the use of customer measurement tools here because they are an important skill set for facility managers. When we talk about measurement instruments, essentially we are discussing the use of questionnaires and other survey formats such as response cards and telephone surveys. As you will read in the next section of this chapter, we feel strongly that all facility organizations should use survey instruments to measure customer satisfaction with FM services. As an example of a customer satisfaction questionnaire, we have included *IFMA's Standardized Facility Management Customer Satisfaction Questionnaire* as Appendix A. We know many facility managers who have used this questionnaire or modified versions of it successfully, and we recommend it to you as a tool to get you started with surveying your customers.

There are common-sense rules for developing measurement instruments like surveys and response cards.

Hundreds of books have been written on the subjects of determining data validity and of using data gathering instruments such as questionnaires and other survey instruments. We would encourage you to read some of those books. While we certainly do not advertise ourselves as measurement experts, regardless of the type of instrument you use, we think there are some common-sense rules to developing measurement instruments and the questions on them. We share these rules with you below.

- Keep your instrument simple. The more direct and the shorter your question can be, the more likely you are going to get a valid answer. If you ask questions that can be answered by a "yes" or "no," you will only have yes and no data. If you are looking for numerical data, then you substitute numerical ratings for the "yes" and "no."

  If you use open-ended questions which start with "How do you feel" or "What do you think" about a service, you will not be force-fitting answers into a "yes," "no," or numerical answer. Your answers will be more subjective.

- Before you try any new data gathering device on a customer population, test it on your staff, the people who will be measured by this device and a sample group of customers. While these steps may be time consuming, they are necessary. You will be surprised that what seemed so plain and straightforward to you will be misinterpreted by those completing the instrument.

- Make certain that each question really gets at the information you want. Think about the answers you will receive and make certain that they are what you want.

- On a survey instrument, if you have no hope or intention of changing a situation, do not indirectly raise false expectations by addressing the issue.

- If you want to measure customer attitudes, use a numerical scale. We personally like a five or six point scale (with the sixth point being not applicable) similar to the one IFMA uses in its questionnaire. Make certain that you define what each of the end points means and, maybe, what you want to be considered average. Usually an odd-numbered scale works best.

- Don't use only one means to measure any factor. For instance, you may want to cross-check complaints about service order performance against questionnaire results for service orders during the same period. Perhaps you also want to follow up on a particularly good or bad project evaluation with a short telephonic survey with the customer representative who completed the evaluations.

- If you are a large organization, as a practical matter, you will need to automate your evaluation results. You may need to enlist the assistance of your information resources organization or an outside professional to help with the processing

Before you use a data gathering instrument, test it on your staff.

If you have no hope or intention of changing a situation, do not raise expectations by asking about it in a survey.

You need to determine how you compare with other comparable FM organizations.

Look for different ways to benchmark. Form a group, find other companies, and use trend data.

end of the survey, but be cautious in working with outside organizations and make sure that you retain control of what data you are going to collect and how the results will be tabulated.

4. Benchmarking or how does your organization measure up?

Benchmarking has become as much a part of the vocabulary of the facility manager as chillers, preventive maintenance and strategic planning. Whether you embrace a formal TQM program or not, there is tremendous value in measuring your organization's performance against others — benchmarking!

Benchmarking for facility managers might take one of several approaches. If you are part of a big organization which has FM departments at other locations, you might compare yourself to them. Or you might compare yourself to large databases gathered by organizations such as IFMA or the Building Owners and Managers Association (BOMA). Depending upon what you want to achieve from benchmarking, you might try to compare yourself against that competitive company that you consider "best-in-class." Finally, you might try to find several companies or agencies which are most like yours and create a benchmarking group. Each of these approaches will produce a different result. For example, if you want to use your benchmarking process as a means and motivator for improvement, you probably would want to benchmark against "best-in-class." If you want to use trend data you might want to consider using the BOMA or IFMA information and measure your organization against their data.

In the same way that these approaches produce different results, they also have different weaknesses. For instance, the association databases both have quality control weaknesses and represent the meshing together of data from varied facilities. (Because BOMA is an older organization, it has a longer track record for minimizing these weaknesses). Benchmarking data which is an amalgam of data from a large number of organizations also does not allow you to follow up with those organizations to find out why you vary from the benchmarks, if you do. One of the most important things to remember when you go through the benchmarking process, and one of your biggest problems, will be reminding your management of this fact. A good example of this was stated by your colleague Frank Yockey of Hewlett Packard, one of our FM quality heros. Frank says, "Don't worry if you aren't even comparable to the organization that you are benchmarking against; I'd be surprised if you weren't different. The heart of benchmarking is understanding the "Why" of that difference and what you want to do about it." [1]

In order to benchmark properly, it is essential that you understand your processes and their direct and overhead costs in detail.

For those who are interested in the benchmarking process, it is absolutely essential that you know which of your services you are going to benchmark and, for each, understand the direct and overhead components of the costs. This sounds basic, but if you have been in an organization that budgets centrally, you may never have computed the true unit costs of providing your services. If you are chargeback funded (your customers pay for service), the allocation rules may well have hidden your true costs of business. Rate setting in a chargeback situation always is a compromise and allocations often represent only an approximation of your true cost for any one service.

A second point we want to make is when defining your services, it is best if you define them roughly the way your benchmarking partners do. If not, you then need to do a lot of data manipulation so that, as much as possible, you are comparing apples to apples and oranges to oranges. Another approach is to not worry about differences in work definition before the benchmarking process. You must then compensate for the differences in definition after the fact when you are analyzing the inevitable "why" of differences for any one benchmark between you and your benchmarking partner. The following example will show the importance of definitions.

You and your benchmarking partner(s) need to speak the same language — apples to apples.

FIGURE 3.5

DEFINITION DIFFERENCES IN BENCHMARKING

Sam Smith, the facility manager for the Wyandotte County Schools, has agreed to benchmark with Mary Brown, the facility manager for a large business school in the same town. One of the benchmarks was to be maintenance and repair costs/sq. ft., a number both could pull out of their budgets fairly easily. Here is what the benchmark included for each of the two organizations.

Sam – Large Multi-Building Public School System	Mary – Single Building Urban School System
Maintenance of buildings and grounds.	Maintenance only above the landlord's standards. No grounds.
Repair of all buildings and FFE Repair projects over $100K capitalized.	Repair of FFE only. No responsibility for major repair.
Custodial service done in-house.	Custodial services contained in the rent.
Gross square footage used for denominator.	Rentable square footage used for denominator.

There probably are three or four other definitional differences. This example shows the difficulties in benchmarking and why merely comparing your unit costs against another's, or particularly against aggregated unit costs such as are found in BOMA and IFMA publications, can really lead to wrong conclusions. This doesn't even address the major issue of what the quality of the services is. Perhaps your company or agency wants to pay for higher quality of custodial services because of your need for a public image, or perhaps you require extended operational hours because your trading room must operate around the clock. Your operations costs naturally will be higher. The real value of benchmarking is in finding better ways of doing your business and in discovering why your unit costs are different from your benchmarking partner's. This value comes from a subjective process, but is dependent upon measurement for its baseline.

Because of the recent interest in FM benchmarking, there has been a great deal written about it. We offer Robert Camp's *Benchmarking*[2] for those of you who want easy-to-understand and implementable benchmarking procedures.

5. *Controlling your processes with statistics*

One of the phrases you will hear time and time again as you read TQM literature is "statistical process control" (SPC). Under SPC, the variability of the process is measured to see 1) if the product or service can be produced within limits, and 2) if the desired value (completed service orders for which materials are available in three working days, for example) can be achieved. By means of SPC, what you might actually find in the FM world is that you are expecting too much of your workers. Without process change, for example, you cannot stay within the limits that you expect nor can you consistently achieve the value you want. This means you have to look at your process to see how, or if, it should be achieved. Maybe your expectations exceed your pocketbook and five days to complete all service orders is all that you can afford, whereas you had arbitrarily set the standard as three days.

SPC can help you if you can reasonably expect a given result from any process.

SPC can become quite sophisticated and specialized depending upon the process you are trying to analyze, so we are not going to go any further with this subject. As a measurement tool, it falls, we think, into that range of knowledge that most of you will never use on a daily basis, but that it is important to be familiar with in anticipation of the time when you need it. If you are particularly interested in SPC, we recommend the work of J. M. Juran[3] or John Ryan,[4] both of whom we found readable. A good overview of SPC, which shows some possible applications for FM, is Barry Lynch's article, "Making Measurement Activities Produce Results," in the July/August 1993 issue of *The Facility Management Journal*.[5]

Measure!

Measure!

Measure!

Please stay with us a little while longer on these measurement tools. We know they are hard and not as stimulating as some of our other discussions, but they are necessary. We'll return to your customers shortly.

No discussion of measurement tools would be complete without exposing you to some of the statistical tools which are commonly used in more formal TQM programs. Whether you choose to use any or all of them is up to you, but they represent yet another set of tools for your tool box. Figure 3.6 defines the standard TQM measurement terms, and Figure 3.7 summarizes the most common statistical terms as they appear in chart form. Then we are finished, honest!

Figure 3.6

Defining TQM Measurement Terms[6]

- Cause and Effect Diagram – Also known as the "fishbone" diagram because of its shape, it is used to examine factors that influence a given situation.
- Flow Chart – A diagram which delineates the way in which a process works.
- Pareto Chart – A chart showing that, in any distribution of data, some contribute in disproportion to the overall effect. The chart is used to determine priorities. It sorts the "vital" from the "trivial."
- Run (Trend) Chart – A chart which shows data over a period of time to look for trends.
- Histogram – A graph showing how frequently something occurs.
- Control Chart – Sometimes called a Shewhart chart, which is used in SPC for testing the statistical significance of data. There are two types of charts depending on the data. One chart is used for data which is measurable such as temperature, pressure, voltage, lengths, etc. The other is used for data which is counted such as typos, mislabeling, etc.
- Scatter Diagram – A graph showing the interrelationship between two variables.

FIGURE 3.7

MEASUREMENT CHARTS AND DIAGRAMS[7]

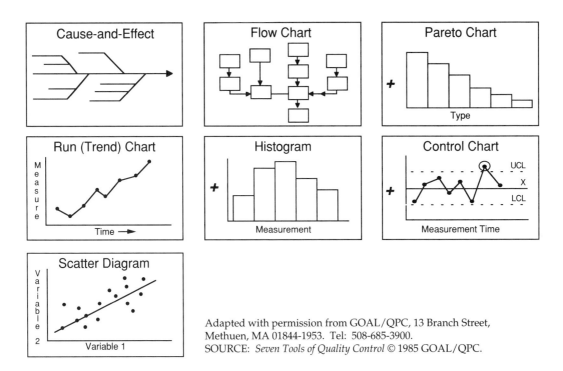

Adapted with permission from GOAL/QPC, 13 Branch Street, Methuen, MA 01844-1953. Tel: 508-685-3900.
SOURCE: *Seven Tools of Quality Control* © 1985 GOAL/QPC.

BACK TO THE CUSTOMERS – THE RATIONALE FOR INVOLVING THEM IN THE MEASUREMENT PROCESS

Despite the fact that this chapter has been oriented towards measurement tools, we need to loop back to the customer, the entity driving our quest for quality. In one of the examples we gave you in the previous section of this chapter, SPC told you that realistically, given your budget, you never would be able to consistently complete all service orders for which you have the materials in less than five days. At the same time, your customer surveys might have told you that your customers expect immediate response on emergency and operational service and three days service on routine service orders. This poses a dilemma which, from our experience, too

Customer involvement in the process arms you with information to talk to management.

Customers need to be aware of why their expectations can or can't be met. You need customer loyalty in a time of shrinking FM resources

Get the picture? Got it! Good!

many facility managers try to solve by only making internal adjustments. Certainly all of you can continually tighten up on your process, but, after a time, you are trying literally to get the "blood out of the turnip." By measuring both your capabilities and your customers expectations, however, you are in a position to approach your management with a recommendation that either management will have to increase your capabilities or better manage customer expectations. Your management owes that to you when you provide them with a logical recommendation based on measurement.

The FM organization alone, however, should not have to defend its position with respect to timeliness, quality and appropriateness of service to top management. Customers of FM organizations can play a critical role in the direction or redeployment of FM resources. As more and more FM dollars are being redirected to activities other than FM by top management in your organizations, your customers need to become aware of why their expectations cannot be met. By developing significant databases on customer expectations and opinions about FM services, your organization can engender loyalty from your customer base, which is critically needed to defend and support against an attempt to diminish your FM resource structure. But, you must have sophisticated baseline data on customers requirements as well as supporting documentation on the success of your service delivery system.

This is why we urge you to go out and get your customers involved in your measurement process. What better way to convince your top management that your services are viewed as essential by your customer population than to have that population tell their top management who tells your top management. GET THE PICTURE? It is some unwritten "law of the hierarchy" which says that top management listens to other top management so use your customers to build your case with their bosses. For example, the word will spread quickly, if you let your customer population know that your management has decided to reduce the cleaning budget and the recycling bins will not be emptied in individual offices more than once per week. If this is unacceptable to your customer population, you better believe that they will let their management know. And who will their bosses talk to? Your boss, of course. That leaves your boss with two choices. He/she either tells you to change the customer perception of their need to have the bins emptied more than once a week (which is highly unlikely), *or* decides that the customer requirement should be met and restores your budget. While we may have oversimplified the case for purposes of illustration, you get the point. You do not have to be a "voice in the wilderness" crying out against the great "FM budget cut injustices." It will work to your advantage to have solid customer data which supports your case and then let your customers do some of the work.

You don't have to "go it alone," if you have customer backing.

TECHNIQUES FOR OBTAINING CUSTOMER DATA

We discussed one way to obtain customer input in our discussion about formal measurement systems above – using questionnaires. Questionnaires are undoubtedly the most scientifically valid means of obtaining customer feedback and we would encourage you to use them about once or twice per year at a maximum. Customers within your companies or agencies are being inundated with questionnaires however, and you have to be careful that the FM questionnaire doesn't end up in the circular file. You need to make use of the questionnaire technique sparingly, but if you haven't obtained baseline data on customer feedback, then by all means start with a questionnaire. Top management also seems to like the idea of a scientific measurement tool such as a questionnaire.

Use questionnaires sparingly!

If you really want to get to know what your customers are thinking, though, we recommend you supplement your questionnaire strategy with other feedback mechanisms. There are several additional tools and tech-

Use other techniques to obtain customer input as well.

niques your authors have used or have heard our colleagues say work well for them and we want to share them with you. The first one is a personal favorite.

FOCUS GROUPS

In the marketing and marketing research fields, the use of focus group interviews is one of the most successful research tools for assessing client service delivery systems. In practice, the use of focus groups has had long-standing reputation as a measure of new product desirability and acceptance. Focus groups have been used traditionally as a mechanism to test new products with targeted potential users prior to mass marketing and advertising campaigns.

During the last ten years with the increased emphasis on customer satisfaction and quality in service businesses, the use of focus groups has become an established mechanism to obtain feedback on service delivery systems.

Some of you may not be all that familiar with focus groups and we should spend a few minutes explaining what they are. A focus group is a group of approximately ten individuals who are representative of your customer populations. When we use focus groups we like to stratify the groups based on the personnel levels within an organization. For example, in one organization we might have focus groups consisting of support staff (secretaries, administrative assistants and clerical personnel), professional staff, scientific staff, technical staff, middle management, senior management and top executives. We have found that grouping the participants with their peers creates a "safe" environment within which to talk and participants tend to open up more than they would in a mixed group. The important thing about a focus group is that the participants have a high comfort level with the process so that they will freely share their true perceptions.

In a focus group a facilitator directs a series of structured questions to the participants and facilitates the discussion. Typically a focus group will start out with

Focus groups allow you to obtain feedback on customer perception of service delivery systems.

Focus groups need outsider facilitation rather than someone from the FM staff.

a very general discussion about an FM service or group of services and then focus on more specific issues as the discussion progresses. We recommend that the FM organization use an outside facilitator rather than someone from the FM department because the tendency is for FM staff to take the discussion about FM services "personally" and they start defending the service and their actions. In fact, it probably is best if FM staff participate only to 1) thank participants, and 2) state a commitment to improvement based on focus group results. It is important for the facilitator to be knowledgeable about the FM world, but impartial about the services. Focus groups can run anywhere from one hour to three hours depending upon the topics which need to be covered and the availability of participants.

For the FM service business, unlike other formal and informal assessment tools such as questionnaires, the focus group method gives you an opportunity to obtain more subjective information from your customers in several critical areas.

1. Perception of service – As you remember from Chapter One, your customers' perception of the quality, timeliness and usefulness of your services is what guides their evaluation of your service delivery capabilities. Although the perception of FM services often is different from their reality, it is the clients' perception that drives their evaluation. A focus group setting allows participants to express their feelings about your services, which is a barometer of their perception.

2. Expectations about FM services – We also told you that every client has a set of expectations about the way your services should be provided. These expectations are subjective and extremely difficult to measure through formal, noninteractive instruments. In a focus group environment participants can discuss service expectations and identify why and how they feel the current level of service deviates from expectations. The service expectations drive the clients' perception of the current levels.

A "quick-fix" solution from a focus group can promote an immediate turn-around in customer perception.

3. Quick-fix solutions – We feel this is the critical factor which makes the focus group technique so valuable. The interactive focus group process typically identifies areas of service where "quick-fix" solutions from a customer perspective can accomplish immediate turn-around in customer perception of service. When customers are asked their opinion about what makes a service excellent, they usually recommend some changes which can be implemented quickly and easily; things which the FM staff may not have considered. If those recommendations are implemented shortly after the assessment process, customers feel they have had an impact on the service delivery system and feel positive about their participation. In other words, THE FM ORGANIZATION ASKED FOR MY OPINION AND LISTENED. This quick-fix outcome of focus groups allows you to demonstrate immediate responsiveness while working on solutions to more difficult problems.

The beauty about focus groups is that while you decide in advance what services you want to include in the discussion, because the sessions are "live" rather than on a printed form, you can change or redirect the flow of discussion. We urge you to consider using focus groups as a supplement to your formal survey instruments.

Because focus groups are "live," you can switch gears if necessary.

RESPONSE CARDS

Of all the comment-type cards that are in use by our FM colleagues, we like the simple response card the best. A response card is simply an abbreviated form of a survey instrument, but it is very short and concise and takes little time for the customer to complete. Response cards are similar to those which you see in restaurants, hotels and other service businesses where you fill them out and leave them in a prescribed place. Response cards are a wonderful tool because you can use them often, modify them frequently to capture different information and they can be distributed by your FM staff as they interact with customers. We have seen them in

A response card is short, concise and takes little time for the customer to complete. Response cards are highly rated by customers.

use in a variety of FM service scenarios which range from housekeeping to space planning. We have used them in all different sizes, shapes, colors and forms in everything from a tent card which folds and can be left on a customer's desk to a card which hangs on the doorknob similar to a "do not disturb sign." The benefit of a response card is that it constantly keeps your organization in touch with the customer by providing timely data. Customers do not mind completing something as brief as a response card and it gives them an opportunity to communicate with your organization on a regular basis. Both our research and that of others suggests that response cards are one of the most effective measurement tools you can use. We have provided you with some samples of response cards here and also in Chapter Six, our Best Practices chapter.

FIGURE 3.8

HOW DID WE DO?

You are an important customer and we value your opinion on how well we are meeting your needs. Please take a moment to answer the following questions. Please rate us: 1 = Excellent 2 = Very Good 3 = Satisfactory 4= Needs Improvement 5 = Poor

Quality of service	1	2	3	4	5
Timeliness of service	1	2	3	4	5
Attitude of staff	1	2	3	4	5
Service met your needs	1	2	3	4	5

Comments: _____

_____

Customer: _____   Room Number: _____

Thank You!

FIGURE 3.9

SERVICE RESPONSE CARD

This is a self-addressed card. Please return it via interoffice mail

Thank You.

Today we completed service no. _____ for you.

We hope that: • We did what you asked for,

• We did it efficiently, and

• We were pleasant and courteous and left your work area clean!

WE VALUE YOU AS A CUSTOMER and we want you to be satisfied. Therefore, we ask you to take a moment to rate our service.

Were YOU satisfied with: (circle one)

	Most satisfied			Least satisfied	
a) How quickly we answered your call?	1	2	3	4	5
b) How we did what you asked for?	1	2	3	4	5
c) Our manner; were we courteous?	1	2	3	4	5
d) How we left your work area?	1	2	3	4	5

Please use the space below for comments (attach a separate sheet, if necessary)

Reprinted with permission from The World Bank

FIGURE 3.10

WERE YOU DELIGHTED?

To help us better serve you, please rate our service and return it to FMS -12.

Quality of Work
- Exceeds Expectations
- Excellent
- Good
- Poor
- Unsatisfactory

Responsiveness
- Exceeds Expectations
- Excellent
- Good
- Poor
- Unsatisfactory

Additional Comments: _____

_____

_____

We thank you for your time and interest.

FIGURE 3.11

WE MISSED YOU!

We're Sorry We Missed You!

The _____ were here at _____ to complete your service order for _____ but were unable to do so.

We'll be back _____ unless we hear from you. If your needs have changed, please contact _____ at _____.

TELEMARKETING

We also have used telemarketing as an effective customer measurement technique. It works best immediately after the service has been provided, while the customer's memory is fresh. It also works best as a means of evaluating a specific service rather than a telephone call to talk about a long list of services in general. A simple phone call after a relocation post occupancy, for example, works extremely well to reas-

Telemarketing is particularly effective to follow-up on the perception of a new or enhanced procedure.

sure the customer that you want to provide the best possible service. You might also try telemarketing after you have issued a new procedure to find out if it makes doing business with the FM organization easier. A telephone call can be an effective follow-up on an unsatisfactory questionnaire or response card. Or, you might use telemarketing to find out how an individual customer liked their new systems furniture. If you don't overdo the use of telephone follow-up and become the FM equivalent of a hated telephone solicitor, it works well for instantaneous feedback.

EVALUATING AND ACTING ON CUSTOMER FEEDBACK

You will commit the ultimate quality sin if you involve your customers in measuring your service quality and then do not act upon their input or provide feedback to them. Having created an expectation level for your customers that your FM organization is committed to listening and incorporating their evaluation into your improvement efforts, you will do irreparable damage if you do not follow through. Your customers want to know that the time they took to fill out a questionnaire, complete a response card, participate in a focus group or complete questions in a telemarketing call was not wasted. You need to close the loop back to your customers by doing one or more of the following:

Follow through! Close the loop with your customers

- Publishing and distributing a report on the results of a major survey;
- Providing feedback on-line through your company E-Mail system or other electronic media;
- Including results from focus groups in a newsletter; and
- Publicly acknowledging changes that came from customers through your measurement efforts.

Remember also to incorporate your results into information you provide to top management. You want to make certain that management knows you are in touch with your customers and are listening to what they tell you.

AND SO IN CONCLUSION...

Realistically, to be a good FM professional, you have to be comfortable with measurement. The good news is that most facility managers, by reason of their training and nature, are comfortable with measuring effectiveness, efficiency, responsiveness and relevancy. The even better news is that most of you, by following our old-fashioned way, can do a more than adequate job of measurement just by understanding a little about statistics, trend analysis, benchmarking, the importance of data, measurement tools and techniques and USING GOOD OLD COMMON SENSE. The danger is in looking only at the statistical approaches to TQM, such as SPC, and getting scared off. We hope we have alleviated your fears.

Common sense prevails.

END NOTES

1. Frank Yockey, Personal communication to the authors.

2. Robert C. Camp, *Benchmarking* (Milwaukee, WI: ASQC Quality Press, 1989).

3. J. M. Juran, *Juran on Quality by Design* (New York: The Free Press, 1992).

4. John M. Ryan, *The Quality Team Concept in Total Quality Control* (Milwaukee, WI: ASQC Quality Press, 1992).

5. Barry Lynch, "Making Measurement Activities Produce Results," *Facility Management Journal*, July/August 1993, pp. 28-34.

6. Mary Walton, *The Deming Management Method* op. cit., pp. 96-118.

7. Ibid.

CHAPTER 4

THE IMPORTANCE OF MARKETING FACILITY SERVICES

MARKETING CONCEPTS AND THEIR RELATIONSHIP TO FACILITY MANAGEMENT

We have spent the past three chapters reinforcing the idea that one of our guiding principles of quality FM is the recognition of the customer as the driver of the process. We have saturated you with the notion that the customer defines service for us. By now, accepting such a role for the customer should be relatively easy; the hard part comes next.

This chapter focuses on the importance of marketing facility services. Does this mean that we want you to "sell" your services to your customers? Do we want you to believe that you actually have to go out and promote what you do in a marketplace? The answer to these questions is yes. That is precisely what facility managers need to do. You may remember in our introduction we said that we must be quality leaders. Well, quality leadership begins with the recognition that facility managers have to assume organizational responsibility for marketing.

Facility managers tend to be a stubborn breed. On more than one occasion we have heard a number of you refute the concept of marketing as critical to the facility business. Facility managers typically respond to the notion of marketing with a slightly tongue-in-cheek response that says, "We have real work to do and do not

We have to assume responsibility for promoting FM services — no one else will!

have time for marketing." You think that marketing is reserved for all those vendor-types, or for your company's marketing department. You can't relate to how their activities come anywhere close to what you need to do.

UNDERSTANDING MARKETING

We have not been trained to market.

The fact is that you couldn't possibly be farther from the truth. Through no fault of your own, you have a basic problem with the concept of marketing. The fault rests with the history of our profession. If you look at most of our academic and on-the-job training programs for facility professionals they do not adequately address the topic of marketing. You spend a fair amount of time on topics such as communications, but do not focus on marketing. It is a void in our professional education and training.

What a truly frightening thought to have to walk the halls and talk to FM customers!

You have a second intrinsic problem with the concept of marketing and that is out and out fear of what it entails. You would like to think that you could practice marketing by Sitting In your Offices (SIO), but the truth of the matter is that you have to get out from behind the safety net of your desks and interact with your customers. We know that for many of you this thought is more terrifying than learning that there is asbestos in the CEO's office. And with good reason. It seems that whenever you do venture out beyond the inner sanctum of your offices, you only get accosted in the halls with news of doom and gloom. When was the last time that you roamed around your building and had someone stop to hand you a note of praise and congratulations? Or, can you remember a meeting with a senior executive of the company which didn't end with ...."Now there's just one more problem I need to tell you about." Facility managers do not have a very good track record when it comes to face-to-face contact with their customers. You need to spend more time "out there" in the customers' world to overcome this fear.

The Fifth Pillar of Quality: there is no such thing as marketing by sitting behind your desk!

MARKETING DEFINED

You can start by accepting what marketing really is. In its pure and simple form, marketing is what you should be doing every day. It is the basic framework for all your facility activities. According to Webster's New World Dictionary, marketing is "all business activity involved in the moving of goods (and services) from the producer to the consumer." It is not strictly sales, although Webster cites sales as a part of marketing, and it is not strictly advertising or promotion, although these too are important components of marketing. It is all business activity that we as facility managers engage in.

Marketing Is Your Strategy and Action Plan for Taking Your Services to Your Customers

It is the rationale behind the way you tell your customers what it is that you do for them as well as the methods you use to get your message across. Marketing is an *M* word which should be incorporated into your quality management efforts.

HOW DO YOU KNOW YOU NEED TO DO MORE MARKETING?

Even if you grudgingly acknowledge that facility managers should be marketers, you may think that you are already doing enough marketing. More often than not, however, when we are applying a test which we have developed as a marketing indicator, we find that facility managers either are not doing enough marketing or the right marketing. As a check to determine whether or not you need to do more marketing, we would urge you to apply the following Three Fives Test.

We have a fail-safe test to determine how well you have been marketing.

THE THREE FIVES TEST

This simple test, proven to be a successful yardstick for measuring the need for marketing, is named the Three Fives Test because it consists of three parts and involves a series of activities dealing with fives. It is a very easy test to apply, and should be administered by the *Senior Facility Official* of the organization. It usually solidifies a facility organization's need to concentrate more on marketing.

PART ONE: RANDOM WALK AND TALK

The first part of the Three Fives Test assesses the employee awareness level of facility services. To administer the test, you need to do two things: 1) walk around the building(s) at random; and 2) stop any five people who work there and ask them the following questions:

Are FM customers aware of services?

1. Do you know who I am?

2. Identify and describe any five services provided by the facility organization.

3. Identify and describe the last five services provided by the facility organization to your department.

SCORING PART ONE.

If four out of the five employees you talk to cannot identify who you are, you have scored poorly. In addition, if four out of five employees cannot describe at least five random services provided by the facility organization in general and five specific services provided to their own organization, you have failed part one of the Three Fives Test. It means that your customer awareness level is extremely low. Your customers do not recognize you as the facilities "guru" and do not know enough about the services your organization provides.

PART TWO: MAINTAIN A TELEPHONE LOG

The second part of the Three Fives Test requires you to maintain a log of the telephone calls from employees that *You Answer Personally* over a five week period. You need to track the following:

Do FM customers call to complain or congratulate?

1. Who the calls come from.

2. The nature of the call.

SCORING PART TWO:

If over the five week period, 50% or more of the calls you receive are from rank and file employees rather than senior managers, you are in trouble. In addition, if 50% or more of the calls are requests for information or complaint calls, you have failed part two of the test. Why? Because it means that you have not done an adequate job of anticipating your mass market's service needs, you do not have sufficient visibility with top management, are not providing services they require, and you do not have a good handle on your customers' evaluation of your service delivery system.

If 50% or more of the calls are to tell you what a good job your staff is doing or how well a service was provided, you receive a gold star. You are on top of your market's needs and must have some type of feedback mechanism for assessing your organization's performance.

PART THREE: MEETING AGENDAS

For the third part of the test, you must do the following:

1. Review the weekly or monthly agendas for executive staff meetings you have attended over a five month period.

How often do you appear as an item on top management's agenda?

SCORING PART THREE:

When you review the agendas, you are looking for the number of times you have made a major presentation or contribution to the substance of the meeting. If you have not provided either of the above to four out of five of those agendas, you should give yourself a poor mark. Why? Because you have not taken a proactive role in these meetings and addressed the value-added benefit of the facility organization's services or the contribution they make to the business bottom line of the company. You have not been heard by top management. You need to do more marketing to senior management in order to reinforce how important the facility organization is to the mission of the company.

Surprisingly enough, even the results of the Three Fives Test do not convince some facility managers of the need to enhance their marketing efforts. If you are one of those who is skeptical and still not convinced, complete the following:

Figure 4.1

Do We Need to Do More Marketing?

1. Has senior management asked you within the past five months to justify current facility costs? _____ Yes _____ No

2. Have you been asked by senior management to lower the costs for any facility services? _____ Yes _____ No

3. Have you been asked by senior management to identify potential service candidates for outsourcing? _____ Yes _____ No

4. Has senior management hinted at or taken action on reducing the size of the facility staff as a cost-cutting measure? _____ Yes _____ No

---

Don't be a skeptic! Take out an FM insurance policy.

If you answered yes to any one of these questions, you need to take the concept of marketing seriously. You need to follow the path of smart managers who see the advantages of marketing the same way they do preventive maintenance on expensive building infrastructure systems and equipment. Marketing is an insurance policy. It is the ammunition you might need in the event that top management decides to make dramatic changes in the way you do business, without your input. Your customers' support might make a significant difference in the way top management views your organization if they are considering resource reduction or redeployment. Your customers may make a difference as to whether or not you have a facility organization.

DEVELOPING A FACILITY MARKETING STRATEGY

Now that we have your attention on the subject of marketing, it is time to concentrate on the mechanics of developing a marketing strategy. In the early days of the FM profession, you had a fairly captive market. In most companies there was only one way to obtain facility services – through the facility organization. You had a monopoly and it was the only service available to the customer. You were in the driver's seat and were able to define your own level of service and your customers accepted it. You dictated how facility services were to be provided and your customers thought they had no choices.

Times have changed dramatically, however. Your market is much more demanding, more knowledgeable and more vocal about what it wants in the way of facility services. Your customers, in many instances, are you conversant as you are with topics such as indoor air quality, energy management, environmental alternatives, Americans with Disabilities Act (ADA), ergonomics and computer aided design (CAD) systems because of mass marketing outside the office environment. These issues no longer are reserved for those of you in the facility business, as they affect your market outside the work environment as well as in the workplace. It is essential for you to develop your own marketing strategy driven by the fact that you have a sophisticated workforce with new and different market demands.

Our market is smarter, more demanding and more cost conscious.

UNDERSTANDING MARKETING STRATEGY COMPONENTS

CUSTOMER AND FACILITY OBJECTIVES

What constitutes our marketing strategy? The first component of any sound marketing strategy is a com-

Know the objectives of the customer and the FM organization before undertaking a marketing program.

plete understanding of two critical objectives:

- The customer organization's overall objective; and
- The facility organization's marketing objective.

Without focusing on the first of these two objectives, the marketing strategy tends to be developed in a vacuum. If you don't know where the customer is headed, you cannot determine where the facility organization should concentrate its efforts. When a customer objective statement is well written, it provides an excellent framework around which to build a facility marketing strategy. To assist you in developing a marketing strategy, you need to look for a customer objective statement which is:

- *Specific* in terms of the core business;
- *Time-related* in terms of parameters for accomplishment; and
- *Measurable* in terms of determining achievement.

The customer objective statement should provide you with guidance on what it sees as its primary business.

The companion piece to the customer objective is a full understanding of what the facility organization is trying to accomplish through its marketing efforts. One of the most serious mistakes an organization can make in undertaking a marketing program is the failure to focus on what its own objectives are for marketing. It is the most significant aspect of a marketing strategy, because it provides a purpose for the organization's plan of action. A well developed marketing objective for a facility organization should address the following:

1. Increasing the awareness of facility services

Have you considered these as your marketing objectives?

As a result of the scoring on the Three Fives Test, you probably realized that you are not doing enough marketing or have not appropriately targeted your marketing efforts. To correct the problem, you will need a marketing strategy designed to heighten the awareness of the services provided by the facility organization. Your customers need to know exactly what services you provide for them.

2. **Decrease the resistance to a particular service, or set of policies and procedures**

As we discussed in Chapter One, one of the hazards of the FM business is that you are consistently in the position of having to tell your customers things they don't want to hear. You are the ones within the company who have to tell employees that they have to pay for coffee after thirty years of thinking free coffee service was an "entitlement," or that you are now going to charge for parking after a long corporate history of no-charge parking. You also are the ones who distribute the office clean-up day missives, the "pack-up-all-your-belongings-late-on-Friday-afternoon-so-that-the-painters-can-paint-your-office" directives and the "due-to-a-scheduled (scheduled by whom your customers ask?)-outage-you-will-not-be-able-to-use-your-computers" announcements. A sound marketing strategy will not alleviate your need to inform your customers of these unpleasantries, but should provide a more effective way to get the message across.

3. **Improve the image of the facility organization as a service provider**

Given what we have described above, it is no wonder you don't always enjoy the "Mr. Nice-Guy" reputation within your companies. You need to develop a marketing strategy which promotes your customer-oriented service philosophy and addresses all the issues of timeliness, appropriateness and quality we stressed in Chapter One. You need a marketing strategy to enhance your image as a counter to the things you have to do which make you unpopular. This is the public relations aspect of your marketing strategy.

4. **Enhance your customers' knowledge about facility services**

There is a big difference between being *aware* of facility services and being *knowledgeable* about them. Again, The Three Fives Test should shed light on whether or not your customers are aware that your services even exist, but you must also detect exactly how much they know

There is a difference between being aware of FM services and being knowledgeable about them.

about the specifics of your services. While it is not necessary for your customers to become facility experts, the more knowledgeable they are about the services you provide, the easier it will be for you to serve them.

5. *Disclose specific qualifications about facility services*

Once more we need to differentiate between our customers' *awareness* and *knowledge* of our services and their understanding of specific *qualifications* required to access the services. As an example, if all employees in your facilities think that length of service is the qualifier for obtaining a parking space next to the main building, then they will not understand why they are ineligible for a space if they have been with the company for ten years and one becomes available. If position in the company is the determining factor for a choice space, then your customers need to know that the only way they will ever be close to the main building is to become a Vice President! Your market needs to know what qualifications they must bring to the table in order to obtain a service or it will forever blame the facility organization for "playing favorites" or treating employees inequitably. Your marketing strategy should address this issue.

To summarize, the marketing strategy formula looks like this:

Marketing strategy =

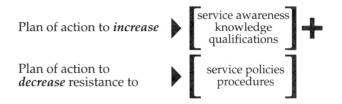

Plan of action to *increase* ▶ [service awareness / knowledge / qualifications] **+**

Plan of action to *decrease* resistance to ▶ [service policies / procedures]

Do your homework on the market first.

MARKET RESEARCH AND ANALYSIS

The second major component of a sound marketing strategy is a thorough analysis of the market. In business terms, market research and analysis is a study of the demand side of the market to learn how to target services which the supply side provides. For us, market analysis is a more comprehensive answer to the question we addressed in Chapter One related to "who are your customers?" You need to develop in-depth information about our customers or your marketplace and also have to identify the direction in which your customers are headed.

You can learn a great deal about your market by concentrating on two factors: 1) the demography or vital statistics of your customers; and 2) the sociology or beliefs, values and interrelationships of your customer organizations. We will spend some time describing each of these factors below.

The demographics of your customers can best be described by the development of customer data on the specific customer populations we discussed in Chapter One.

A valuable exercise is the development of customer profiles which can be shared with the customer as an indicator of the facility organization's commitment to assist its customer in furthering the business mission. A customer profile can be a marketing tool which is provided to the customer as a deliverable. Developing a market profile takes a considerable amount of research on the part of a facility organization and requires access to information which only the customer may be able to provide. For this reason, as well as furthering the idea of "partnering" with your customer, the customer profile should be developed jointly with the customer. We recommend that you negotiate the data elements of your customer profile with your customer. In the first place it is a "good-faith" effort on your part to demonstrate to the customer that you are trying to develop a document that is not only useful to the facility organization, but to the customer as well. In the second place, a customer profile should be tailored to the specific customer population, as some data elements may not be universally applicable to all customers. For instance, with the real estate data element described below, some

Become a partner with your customer and develop a Customer Profile that meets your needs and those of your customer.

customers (or business units) may have their own port-folio of buildings for which you provide asset manage-ment. In addition to the data you would want to gener-ate for your own organization, your customer may have additional requirements they would like you to incor-porate.

While we would encourage you to develop detailed data elements for inclusion in your customer profiles with your customers, from our experience, customer profiles should contain the following data at a mini-mum:

DEMOGRAPHIC DATA

Data elements of your customer profile.

- *Size and diversity of the market*

  This represents data elements in two areas: 1) size of the market in terms of the overall numbers of employees in the organization; and 2) make-up of the market in terms of diversity of position category (administrative, scien-tific, manufacturing, management, executive, etc.). It is important to know how many people you are dealing with and how they are distributed among occupational categories.

- *Characteristics of facilities*

  This data needs to be tailored to each individual cus-tomer. Some customers may have a real estate portfolio comprised of office, manufacturing, warehouse and spe-cial purpose space. You will want to develop a profile of the specific type of space each customer occupies, owns and/or leases. You will want to have information on the organizational distribution of staff by building, i.e. are organizational units co-located or dispersed among build-ings; fair market value of the buildings; building audit information by major infrastructure system; and un-usual characteristics or features of the building.

- *Expenditures on facility services*

  This data element identifies the size of the market in terms of dollars available to spend on facility services and should be broken out by service category and by building. If your organization provides facility services gratis to the customer, it is important for the customer to have an historical perspective on the magnitude of facility expenditures and how they have been allocated across service areas and specific buildings. It becomes an even more critical element if you are currently using or considering using a charge-back system for facility services. You and your customer need to know how much they have been spending and what constitutes their service priorities.

- *Age distribution of market*

  While some might consider this to be a discriminatory indicator, we have found it to be a particularly useful indicator of facility service preferences. Facility organizations using this as a data element have found that it tells them a great deal about the types of services they may need to provide in the future. For example, if the age distribution of your customer group is at the young end of the spectrum, say in the 22 to 30 range, when you couple this with the sociological data described below, you may learn a great deal about the kind of fitness facility you will need to provide. You may find that your population is demanding much more active exercise facilities equipment and services than an older population, which may be demanding less strenuous activities.

- *Educational distribution of market*

  This indicator is similar to the age data element. Educational information on your population will provide you and your customer with valuable insight into their work environment requirements. If your workforce is comprised mostly of Ph.D.-types in computer science, you will know that their requirements will be completely different than a workforce with widely diversified educational backgrounds.

- *Rate of growth or shrinkage of market*

  You also will need to know if your customer population is growing or if it is slated for a "downsizing" effort. Once you know the key characteristics of the population and if it is expanding or contracting, you will be in a better position to determine your service strategy for that organization. As an example, if organization X is a "high demand" organization in terms of certain facility services which are expensive to provide, when you learn that the organization is scheduled for downsizing you will know that you will be scaling back your service level to that customer population.

We have provided a sample customer profile format, using the data elements described above, which we have used successfully for facility organizations.

FIGURE 4.2

DATA ELEMENTS FOR A CUSTOMER PROFILE

I.   Customer Vision Statement

II. Customer Objective Statement

III. Customer Organization Demographics
   A. Size and Diversity of Market
       • Organization structure (chart)
       • Total number of employees
       • Number of employees by occupation code (administration, scientific, manufac-turing, professional, etc.)
       • Age distribution (by occupation code)
       • Educational distribution (by occupation code)
   B. Rate of Growth or Shrinkage
   C. Niche Markets (see next section)

IV. Real Estate Demographics
   • Physical location of customer building(s) (map)
   • Number of buildings occupied by customer
   • Square footage per building occupied by customer
   • Distribution of occupation codes by building and floor
   • Square footage and building distribution of leased space
   • Square footage and building distribution of owned space
   • Fair market value of owned buildings
   • Distribution and square footage of space by facility category (office, manufacturing, R and D, warehouse, computer, etc.)
   • Space allocation by occupation code (density)
   • Churn rate

V. Customer Expenditures on Real Estate and Facility Services
- Rent (by building)
- Relocation
- Design
- Construction
- Utilities
- Operations and maintenance
- Alterations
- Housekeeping
- Grounds maintenance/landscaping
- Security
- Telephone
- Telecommunications
- Printing
- Reproduction
- Graphics
- Mail and distribution
- Conference room scheduling
- A/V services
- Motor pool, shuttle bus, chauffeur services
- Courier
- Office services
- Word processing
- Travel services
- Food services

VI. Customer Sociological Data and Trends
  A. Value Indicators
  B. Environmental Concerns
  C. Alternative Work Styles
   - Telecommuting
   - Hoteling
   - Job sharing
   - Flex time
   - Compressed work week
  D. Work Environment
   - Formal
   - Informal
  E. External Customer Interaction

VII. Customer Funding Mechanism(s) for Real Estate and Facility Services

VIII. Customer Real Estate and Facility Service Requirements

IX. Customer Competitive Market Analysis
   A. Industry Trends
   B. Market Growth or Shrinkage
   C. Target Market(s)
   D. Major Competitors
   E. Best-in-Class Benchmarks
X. Additional Data Elements Requested by Customer

NICHE MARKETS

Target markets are small segments of your overall customer population.

A component of your demographic customer profiles should be an analysis of any specialized market segments or niche markets within the overall customer population. Niche markets are segmented populations which may require specialized attention or have service needs which are separate and apart from the larger customer unit. Examples of niche markets within your company might include:

- *Marketing staff:* The company's marketing department, given their external demands, might dictate unusually fast turnaround of certain services such as reproduction, graphic and photographic services and they will not tolerate anything less. You might also learn that they work independently and, therefore, may want more one-on-one attention than an organization which tends to work in a team atmosphere. You might find that they are on the road most of the time and are not as concerned with the physical environment of the office as they are with the capabilities for high-tech linkages outside the office such as mobile phone and fax service, interconnectivity of lap-top PC's, international telephone numbers, etc.

- *R and D staff:* The demands on an R and D staff by senior management may dictate to you a facility requirement of flexible space configuration. Often, the R and D community may be working on a project which is constantly changing and their workspace may need to reflect this. In order for them to be responsive in their jobs, they may need to reconfigure their work area on a frequent basis and may want you to design a work area which provides them with the flexibility to change it themselves. They may not want to have to call the facility organization every time they need to change the way they are working.

- *Legal department*: The legal department may be handling proprietary or intellectual property for the company and may have security requirements that go above and beyond what other organizations require. They may have "red robe rooms" which require highly specialized security measures.

- *High-tech groups*: Some organizations have a highly technical group of folks who have working habits which may be different than the traditional 9 to 5 work day. Many of these folks work around the clock and may need accommodations within their work area to handle an almost "live-in" arrangement. They also may have excessive needs for power, lighting, etc.

- *Senior executives*: The majority of senior executives within any company will require special attention in the area of "concierge" services. Senior executives may require chauffeur services, catering, courier services and other services which may not be offered to the overall population of the company.

You need to know what these niche markets are and how you will have to target services to meet their needs.

SOCIOLOGICAL DATA

Sociological data is as important to the development of your customer profiles as the hard data on their demographics. Focusing on the sociological aspects of your customer organization allows you to study the social and cultural environment of your customers and to be aware of trends that are taking place throughout the company as a whole and within specific business units. You will want to do trend data analysis to answer questions such as:

Trend data on the market helps to understand your customer's sociological needs.

- Is the company becoming more environmentally aware?
- Are they demanding recycling programs?

- Are they conscious of indoor air quality?

- Are they looking for creative uses of alternative products which have positive environmental by-product applications?

- Is the customer population heavily dependent on technology?

- Is the customer population moving towards alternative work styles such as hoteling, telecommuting, job sharing, etc.?

- How does the workforce interact? Do they perform most of their work in teaming arrangements or on an individual basis?

- Is senior management of the customer organization highly interactive with the workforce or do they maintain an executive-level distance from their employees?

- Does the organization tend to have a formal or informal atmosphere?

- Is the organization highly interactive with the public or external customers?

Where is your customer headed?

You are trying to answer the questions related to "where your customers (as an organizational unit) are headed." It is important for you to know about their organization culture because it affects the way in which you provide service to them. You need to know what the organizational tolerances are in order to be able to negotiate service standards with them that will meet their specific requirements. The rationale for looking at the sociological aspects of your customer population is to make certain that you know how the individuals within the organizational unit relate to each other and to the facility staff and where they see themselves headed as an organization.

COMPETITIVE ANALYSIS

The renewed emphasis on quality that has been sweeping the country over the past several years has resulted in the realization that the facilities business is competitive and services must be marketed. We are living in an age of outsourcing which has become a fact of facilities life. If your competition, which in this case usually means an outsourcing firm, knows that their services must be marketed, shouldn't you know what these firms are saying to your customers about providing facility services?

Now we don't want you to get the impression that we are against outsourcing. Quite to the contrary, we see it as the facility manager's responsibility to identify opportunities for achieving savings and enhanced service through outsourcing and promote them to top management before top management dictates a less desirable outsourcing arrangement. You cannot bury your heads in the sand and try to hide from outsourcing; rather you should turn it to your advantage where it is appropriate.

Don't fight outsourcing. Be out in front by knowing when it is appropriate and what the firms are offering your customers.

In this age of outsourcing it is important for you to maintain a competitive advantage wherever possible in order to make your customers want to do business with your organization rather than with someone else. As an example, if a Group Vice President tells an organization to reduce its expenditures on administrative or real estate services, and the bottom line is that they can get the same quality service for less by contracting with a firm other than the facility organization, they will, *unless* you have demonstrated to them that there is value-added by doing business with you. While you may not be able to lower the cost of providing the same service a vendor provides, if you have adequately performed your market analysis and know that an organization is willing to pay a premium for enhanced response time, personal attention, etc., then your customer may be able to persuade the Group Vice President that the higher costs are justifiable. In order to do this you must know what the competition has to offer to ensure that your customers are comparing apples to apples as part of their decision making process. The bottom line is that you do not want to encounter any surprises from a potential outsource alternative that you are not prepared to address.

Stay on top of the competition.

APPLYING MARKETING TECHNIQUES

With all this body of knowledge about your customer populations, you probably are wondering when we will get to some hands-on applications of marketing techniques. If we were losing some of you, hopefully this next section will stimulate your interest. In the facilities business you can learn some valuable techniques from standard marketing practice. Review these techniques with your staff and determine how they can be applied within your own company.

TECHNIQUE ONE: STAY AHEAD OF MARKET NEEDS

Predict your customers' needs before they have to tell you.

By now, if you have followed even a little bit of our guidance, you have collected a wealth of data on your customer population. You have market data on demographics, niche markets and sociological factors, as well as data on customer satisfaction through surveys, focus groups and response cards. With all this information you ought to be able to stay ahead of what your market needs. For example, if you have market information that tells you that every year department Y grows or shrinks by a certain number of employees and that the department head will ask for space like clockwork, let your space management staff approach the department before he contacts them.

Know your point of sale.

In marketing terms, to predict your market needs, you need to know where an appropriate "point of sale" should be. You may have learned that it is time-consuming for employees of a particular business unit to go to the supply store to pick up supplies. Make the point of sale easy for them and have a supply cart stocked with standard office products stop at these organizations twice a day. Another example would be having a handyman cart roam the buildings and stop at scheduled intervals within organizational units. The handyman cart would carry light bulbs, tools for small repairs and other "quick-fix" items to allow a handyman to take care of several problems at one time. This makes the point of sale come to the customer and allows the facility staff to aggregate its response calls, rather than handling them one at a time

One final example would be to provide one-stop-shopping for services which customers traditionally have had to go off-premise to handle. If your company is losing productive time from its employees because they leave the premises to do errands such as pick up laundry, go to the bank, make travel arrangements, etc. have these services located within your facilities. Make the point of sale easy for the customer by predicting their needs and responding to them in advance of a request.

TECHNIQUE TWO: PREPARE THE MARKET FOR CHANGE

Just as you do not want to be surprised by a competitive facility services provider, your customers also do not want surprises from their facility organization. They want continuous feedback and information on what you are planning to do within their work environment. Traditional marketing practices support an ongoing campaign approach to keeping customers informed about what will be happening to them. Let's look at some practical examples.

Make certain there are no surprises.

There is nothing worse than having the facility organization tell a customer organization on Thursday afternoon that it is time for the cyclical painting of their area. What a way to antagonize your customers. Customers do not like to be "surprised" by a short-sighted announcement that the facility organization probably knew about for months and months. What is worse, you typically aggravate the situation by telling them that it was "scheduled cyclical painting." Scheduled by whom? How to ruin your credibility with your market.

Another good example is the need for a change in the way they have been doing business with you, a change which you spring on them at the last minute. Suppose they have had a standard procedure for initiating a work

Test market your changes before they affect everyone.

request and you are going to change it. Typically, you have a tendency to announce the change five minutes before you are about to implement it. This does not endear you to your customers. Instead of jumping into a major change, why not do what standard market practice calls for and do a test market of the procedure. Test the new procedure with an organizational component with whom you have a good relationship and work the bugs out before you implement it for the universe. If you have a good relationship with this customer group, they will help you smooth out the rough spots before you have to go "public" with the change. You will be happy with the end result and your customer groups will be pleased with a smooth transition. Compliments all around!

TECHNIQUE THREE: STIMULATE MARKET INTEREST IN FACILITY ACTIVITIES

Keep FM customers on the edge of their seats for what you are doing next.

If any of our readers are "vintage"(like we are) you will remember the old Burma Shave® signs that made those long road trips with our parents tolerable. You also will recall that while their primary purpose was to advertise the Burma Shave® product, the manner in which they did that was to "titillate" the market. They provided their market with little snippets of information on each sign which built upon one another until the final message appeared. Not only did they stimulate your interest in their product, but you looked forward to the clever little sayings. Why can't you do the same thing in your business?

Let the market become your advocate.

If you are going to do a major construction or renovation project in a wing or corridor of a building, have a series of signs which provide your customer with information on the nature of the project. Or, if you are constructing a new facility, make a time-lapsed video which can be displayed in the lobby of your building for all customers to watch. Your customers would love to be "sidewalk" superintendents and you can use this technique by providing customers with peepholes to view the behind-the-scenes activity of a construction effort. If you stimulate your market's interest in a project, they will be your biggest supporters and will serve as an advocate for future efforts.

TECHNIQUE FOUR: CREATE OPPORTUNITIES FOR SHOWCASING FACILITIES WORK

Tooting your own horns is the point of this technique. Not only are facility managers a stubborn lot, but you also are extremely modest. You don't like to talk about your successes; you take a fairly dim view of patting yourselves on the back. Well, good market practice tells us that you should be your own promoters and create opportunities to highlight the good works you have done.

Suppose you have a building which is about to celebrate a significant occasion – say, a 25th birthday. A birthday celebration is something most organizations can relate to because they typically do something special (in the way of cakes, balloons, etc.) for groups of their employees. Why not suggest to top management that you hold a minor birthday celebration for your building and create a diorama of the changes that have taken place in the building over its life. You can use photos, which you probably have in your archives, to show the upgrades and retrofits which the facility organization has overseen in the building as the company's needs have changed. Top management could set aside a time to have a cake and invite employees to attend a small celebration. *Voila*! The facility organization is in the spotlight and you have an opportunity to showcase how you have maintained and preserved one of the company's biggest assets over the years.

Highlight your FM accomplishments; don't keep them hidden.

On a less dramatic scale, suppose you have developed an excellent recycling program for your headquarters building which top management has decided should be implemented in regional locations. In most companies, top management would have some other organization be responsible for getting a similar program off the ground. Step up to the challenge. Develop an imple-

Look for opportunities to be in the spotlight.

mentation kit which provides a region with a step-by-step approach for establishing a similar program, **and** outline a "dog and pony" show which one of your staff would take on the "road" to provide technical assistance. You have demonstrated your ability to market your "product" as well as the capability to deliver technical assistance.

Let's face it, given everything else a company does, promoting the facility organization probably does not rank high on anyone's list. This task falls to you and you must seek and often create opportunities for your services to take center stage.

CREATING A FACILITY MARKETING TOOL KIT

In addition to the techniques we outlined in the section above, we also would like to leave you with a "tool kit" of practical ideas which seem to work well for most facility organizations.

A FACILITY MARKETING PACKAGE

Other organizations within your company are familiar with marketing packages; why shouldn't the facility organization have one? We think you should have a professional-looking, generic marketing package which is given to each and every employee in the company. It would contain information such as:

- Building(s) map(s);

- Location of organization business units (or departments) within each building;

Make it easy for your market to know you. Give new employees a comprehensive FM package.

- Service directory which includes a brief description of the key services provided by the facility organization and appropriate telephone numbers for the lead people on each service;

- Service standards for the base level of service which everyone in the company receives;

- Hard copies of forms such as work requests which

customers would use (even if they access services on-line through a computer network);

- Cut sheets on things the facility group is doing for the company such as ergonomics for computers, indoor air quality, recycling programs, etc.; and

- Results of customer satisfaction surveys you have taken.

Once you have this wonderful package, do not make the mistake of some facility organizations — they turn it over to the Human Resource Department which provides new employee orientation. **If** your package is going to be used at orientation, have the senior facility official give a little talk and hand out the packets personally. First, this provides the name recognition (so you don't have to do as many part one's of the Three Fives Test!), and two, it allows you to get the employee off to a proper start with the facilities group. If you are developing a package for the first time and need to distribute it to all employees of your company, arrange to have small all-hands meetings with each organizational unit to personalize the distribution of the packages and provide exposure for the facility organization.

Sit and talk with top executives on a regular basis.

Closed Circuit TV

Many companies have an in-house television network capability, which is an excellent vehicle for facility marketing efforts. You may want to establish your own weekly "fireside chats" to review facility activities with the entire company or target specific organizational units with certain messages. Closed circuit TV also is an excellent vehicle to promote a particular facility-sponsored event such as national safety week, environment day, ecology day, etc. Using this vehicle allows you to provide consistent information on a variety of topics to large populations all at the same time.

Make TV a medium for communication.

Visitations to Senior Management

Some of you may draw the line here! You may be thinking, these authors want us to be television stars, develop extensive data banks on our customers, be in the birthday party business **and** make regular visits to senior management. You probably think we are crazy and if you do all these things you never will get any work done. Well in case you have forgotten our message, THIS IS YOUR WORK. This is what you should be doing.

We hate to say this, but one of the most successful marketing techniques is for the senior facility official to make routine visits to the company's top executives. These visits should be scheduled regularly and you should have a fairly structured agenda when you meet with these folks. During these visits you should devote a portion of the time to providing the executives with "heads-up" information on facility issues which concern them and their departments, as well as time for them to give you a status report on service. Some of the time also should be dedicated to having them provide insight on any new developments in their area which might involve the facility organization in the future.

Information Sharing with the Market

Keep your market informed. Share, share, share!

Facility organizations which are successful in their marketing efforts take great pride in the amount of information they disseminate to their customers. Many organizations send out a regular newsletter via electronic mail or hard copy which talks about the work of the organization and highlights some of its people. Other facility organizations distribute FYI-grams whenever there is a change in policy or procedure. Still other organizations hold "press conferences" to talk about changes or introduce new facility services.

If the above tool kit does not meet your needs, develop your own using the guide we have developed.

FIGURE 4.3

MARKETING TOOL KIT

1. What do we need in our marketing package?
   - Building maps
   - Company directory by Business Unit/Department and building location
   - Facilities service directory
   - Key facilities telephone numbers
   - Customer service/help desk/hot line number
   - After hours number
   - Emergency numbers
   - Service standards
   - Sample or hard copies (completed) of forms

   _____

   _____

   - Special program cut sheets
     - ___ ergonomics   ___ recycling
     - ___ work stations   ___ indoor air quality
     - ___ systems furniture   ___ energy management
     - ___ ADA   ___

   - Other cut sheets

     _____   _____

     _____   _____

   - Customer evaluation data
     - ___ surveys/questionnaires
     - ___ response cards
     - ___ focus group results
     - ___ interviews

     _____

     _____

- Other information

  _____   _____
  _____   _____
  _____   _____
  _____   _____
  _____   _____

2. How should we distribute marketing packages?
   - Drop offs
   - All-hands meetings
   - On-line
   - New employee orientation
   - Special locations within buildings
   - Other

   _____
   _____
   _____
   _____

3. How should we communicate with our customers?
   - Videos
   - Closed circuit TV
   - Fairs
   - Newsletters
   - FYI-grams
   - On-line
   - Personal visits
   - Building tours
   - Walk the halls
   - Orientation
   - Staff meetings
   - Other

   _____
   _____
   _____

DEVELOPING A MARKETING PLAN

By now your eyes have glazed over on the subject of marketing and you are wondering when this chapter will be over! The end is near. We only have to translate the concepts, techniques and tools into a formal plan and we will be on the home stretch. Stay with us, however, since this plan is an important ingredient in your recipe for success. Without a plan of action, all your good ideas related to marketing will never come to fruition.

The marketing plan is your guidance document for taking many of the activities we identified in this chapter and in previous ones, and applying them to your interactions with customers. To accomplish all this, you need to have a fairly ambitious plan or series or plans. Our recommendation is to develop a single plan which governs your marketing efforts for the company as a whole and individual plans based on the way in which you have organized your market for service delivery, i.e., by business unit, department, geographic region or building complex.

You will remember earlier in this chapter we talked about the need to identify your organization's strategic goals with respect to marketing and we listed the following as minimal:

- Anticipating and meeting the company's overall objective and those of individual business units;

- Increasing the awareness of facility services;

- Decreasing the resistance to service changes, policies and procedures;

- Improving the image of the facility organization;

- Enhancing the customers' knowledge about facility services; and

- Disclosing specific qualifications about facility services.

We consolidated these objectives and translated them into four major tasks which we feel would be appropriate as a starting point for any marketing plan. Our components for a basic marketing plan are:

1. Conduct market research

As we have said repeatedly, you need to have hard data on who your customers are, what their requirements are and where they are headed. You want to collect and maintain baseline data on your customer populations in order to compile both corporate and specific business unit customer profiles. This is the starting point for your marketing plan. If you do not have the demographic, sociological and market segment data we have talked about in this chapter, you will not know enough about your customers to serve them adequately.

Another component of your market research is the analysis of your competitors to make certain that there are no surprises waiting for you at some point in the future. You will learn a fair amount about what your competitors are offering by staying in touch with your customers, but you also need to maintain additional information on what is being offered in the facilities market outside your own company.

2. Promote facility services

We have stressed this over and over. You need to take proactive steps to make certain you and your facility organization are visible, as well as measures to ensure that your customers are knowledgeable about the services you provide.

3. Keep customers informed

As you recall, we talked about information dissemination and feedback on a variety of topics. Your customers want information on new or improved services, they want information on changes in policies and procedures in advance of implementation, they want information on facility service trends which may impact the way they do business in the future and they want feedback on service delivery evaluation information they provided to you. Customers are information junkies! As part of your marketing plan, you need to target specific actions to ensure that customers have all the information they want and need.

4. Evaluate service delivery

This is the tie-in back to Chapter Three and the discussion of measurement and evaluation. It is the task for maintaining the integrity of your marketing plan and the task that ensures that you not only are delivering quality services, but that your marketing program is of the highest quality as well. You must evaluate your services, but at the same time you must also evaluate the way you promote them. The evaluation task closes the loop in the marketing plan to make it a continuous process — one of the underlying principles of quality management.

What is a marketing plan?
Your guidance document.

When we look at the four components of our marketing plan as a continuous process, we also see the quality managment process at work.

Promote Services

Conduct Market Research

Keep Customers Informed

Evaluate Service Delivery

Taking the four tasks outlined above as the framework of a marketing plan, we have provided a simple format which may assist you in the process of identifying your own specific action steps. For our sample plan we have listed action steps which would be appropriate for a hypothetical facility organization and left a column for you to fill in for your own organization.

Figure 4.4

MARKETING PLAN

Task	Hypothetical Facilities Organization	Your Facilities Organization
1. Conduct Market Research	• Three Fives Test	_____
	• Focus Groups	_____
	• Surveys	_____
	• Interviews	_____
	• Annual Reports	_____
	• Industry Trends Analysis	_____
	• Competitive Analysis	_____
2. Promote Services	• Marketing Packages	_____
	• Employee Orientation	_____
	• Videos	_____
	• Closed Circuit TV	_____
	• Visitations	_____
	• Presentations	_____
	• Events	_____
	• "Walk and Talk"	_____
3. Keep Customers Informed	• Newsletters	_____
	• FYI-Grams	_____
	• Exhibits	_____
	• Focus Groups	_____
	• Visitations	_____
	• Press Conferences	_____
	• All-Hands Meetings	_____
4. Evaluate Service Delivery	• Telemarketing	_____
	• Surveys	_____
	• Response Cards	_____
	• Interviews	_____
	• Focus Groups	_____

MARKETING TO TOP MANAGEMENT: KNOWING YOUR AUDIENCE AND THEIR AGENDA

We cannot leave this topic without spending some time on the subject of top management. Marketing to individuals at the most senior levels of your company requires not only a thorough understanding of their organizational position within the company, but also a refined sense of their agenda.

Top management comes in various forms; some are real estate oriented, some are heavily into human resources, while others are geared towards dollars and cents.

We hear from our colleagues time and time again that one of the most difficult tasks they face is communicating with senior management of the company. If you apply the third part of the Three Fives Test and learn that that you have not been active or vocal in senior staff meetings, you will be fully aware of what we mean when we say it is tough to make top management stop and listen to those of us in the facilities business.

You have spent the better part of your lives as facility managers trying to make your senior management understand what you do and how important it is. This is part of the reason you have failed in the past to "get their attention." No one in a top management job (or any other job for that matter) wants to hear why you think *your* function is so important; they want to know how it relates to the importance of what *they* do. Instead of trying to prove that you are an important component within the company in your own right, you should be demonstrating how you contribute to the core competency of the company and its bottom line. To do this you need to understand the agenda of the person in charge.

Where does your top management fit in this picture?

If you are to succeed in maintaining open communication with top management within your company, you have to understand what makes them tick. Reporting to a Vice President for Human Resources is quite different from reporting to a Vice President for Real Estate. Their management responsibilities are different and so is their management agenda. It is necessary for you to know where you and your organization fit into that agenda.

Take for example a Vice President for Human Resources. A typical Vice President for Human Resources is responsible for personnel issues, usually quality management and/or TQM, dealings with unions, the company training programs, and anything else that concerns the *people* within a company. The rationale for having the facility organization report to this function is that facilities have an impact on the work environment of the people. If you report to this person, you will have to be aware that the individual's agenda probably will be more focused on customer service, the health and welfare of the employees in terms of environmental issues, motivation, etc. If you want to be successful in communicating and marketing to this person, you will need to make certain that you discuss facility issues within this context.

Some facility organizations report to a Vice President for Administration. This individual typically has a broad scope of responsibility which may range from human resources, to management information systems to contracting and finance. Individuals in these positions will be interested in streamlining contracts, the advantages of outsourcing, financial bottom lines and a wide variety of issues.

Facility organizations reporting to Vice Presidents for Real Estate have a completely different agenda to learn. Most of these individuals are square footage oriented and want to know how costs relate to square footage numbers. For the most part they are BOMA-oriented and will have a more difficult time dealing with value-added services. Their whole frame of reference is real estate based and it will be necessary to approach your communication and marketing strategy with this in mind.

The key here is to do your homework and identify what the hot buttons are for your senior management. Knowing what their agenda is will dictate, to a certain extent, how you interact with them both in terms of substance of the materials you present and format that you use. We have developed a checklist which has

proven useful in determining how to market to top
management.

FIGURE 4.5

MARKETING TO TOP MANAGEMENT

1. *The FM organization reports to:*
   - Vice President/Director Administration
   - Vice President/Director Real Estate
   - Vice President/Director Property Management
   - Vice President/Director Human Resources
   - CFO
   - other   _____

2. *This individual's background is:*

   _____
   _____
   _____
   _____ _____
   _____

3. *The major issues on this individual's agenda include:*
   - contract streamlining
   - TQM
   - downsizing
   - outsourcing
   - ADA
   - indoor air quality
   - customer service
   - employee relations
   - union negotiations
   - other   _____

4. *This individual's preferences for communications/presentation include:*
   - budget information/hard facts and figures
   - briefing books/memos

- memos in bullet form
- weekly one-on-one meetings
- informal telephone conversations to "chat" on issues
- structured reports
- other _____
  _____
  _____
  _____

5. I meet or talk with this individual:
- once a day
- once a week
- once a month
- once every quarter
- once every six months
- once a year
- other _____
  _____

6. My strategy for strengthening my ability to communicate/market to this individual includes:

_____
_____
_____
_____
_____

Before we leave the subject, we want to remind you that marketing needs to become part of your strategic approach to the delivery of FM services. It should be seen as an integral part of the FM process and one for which you as the facility manager are responsible for taking the lead.

We will move to our discussion of continuous improvements and our suggestions for you with regard to your leadership role.

CHAPTER 5

THE CONCEPT OF CONTINUOUS IMPROVEMENT

DEVELOPING THE CONTINUOUS IMPROVEMENT ETHIC

We have come full circle with this book and want to end our discussion on quality FM by talking about the concept of continuous improvement. Unless the entire facility organization, from the facility manager down to the person who is in the maintenance and repair group, or the person unloading boxes on the loading dock, takes pride in their contribution to the facilities, you will sub-optimize the quality of FM. Many of the old-fashioned principles of quality management are attitudinal. In fact, they do not cost anything to implement directly, which is one of the reasons they are so popular. Instilling that attitude can only be done by you, the facility manager, over the long run. You reward those who display pride in workmanship and you retrain those who don't do things right the first time. Most important is that you don't punish those who did it right, but in doing so, took slightly longer or caused the unit cost to go up. This means you have to change your attitude too. Your employees will be carefully observing you to see what happens the first time that producing a quality FM service runs up against time or funding constraints...and you all know it will.

No single attitude is as important as convincing everyone in the organization that you truly want them to

Many of the old-fashioned principles of quality FM are attitudinal.

Second Pillar of Quality: Commitment to continuous improvement.

do things right the first time. Many of your FM staff have been trained, due to the press of time and budget, that what management really wants is for them to accomplish any task, from alterations to maintenance to repair, at the absolutely minimally acceptable level in the quickest possible time. As an example, we have seen facility staff come to an area for a repair (when we have been customers) and do only what was absolutely necessary to get us back on line despite the fact that the job neither looked good nor stood much chance of remaining fixed for the long run. To these repairers, our needs were just another ticket to be cleared and they were "straight" with their management provided they did not spend over $50 on our repair. What kind of attitude does that engender in that worker? How can that person have any pride in workmanship?

What happened to the idea of pride in workmanship?

This phrase, *pride in workmanship,* is one of the key phrases to support our notion that quality FM is an old-fashioned concept. What ever happened to the idea of instilling pride in workmanship? Are there factors other than the press of time and budget that have been working against the concept of pride of workmanship? While we do not want to lean too heavily on the manufacturing analogy, we want you to think for a moment about how many years we were waiting until the end of the assembly line before we inspected for quality and then cast off the rejects to be reduced to scrap or reworked. The Japanese, primarily, taught us that such a procedure was tremendously wasteful of both labor and material and that the best process was to instill pride of craftsmanship during manufacturing so that companies didn't need a herd of inspectors at the end of the line culling the product.

Just think of the costs to your organization of repeat calls (do you track the repeat calls and try to reduce them?) or of the water damage because a leak was not truly fixed the first time. The same is true of instilling pride of service in your designers and engineers, in your mailroom or at your switchboard. Pride of craftsmanship has a slightly different meaning in each function of

FM, but no single principle can produce a more beneficial attitude in your organization and its reputation within your company or agency.

Pride in craftsmanship soon is transferred to pride in facilities, and your staff start taking proprietorship. When this happens, all employees of the company or agency start taking pride in the facilities. Individuals who are proud also are happy and will do amazing things. When your craftsman knows that you count on him or her, most will come through and do the right thing, even in the absence of instruction. That then forms the basis for an empowered organization. "Management that is interested in raising dividends will take immediate, decisive steps to...remove the barriers that stand between the production worker and his pride of workmanship."[1]

Staff need to take proprietorship for the facilities.

WHAT ABOUT THE FACILITY MANAGER'S ATTITUDE? — THAT TRANSLATES INTO LEADERSHIP

Focusing on your customer and instilling pride of workmanship are both largely attitudinal and must be done primarily through the leadership of the facility manager. Attitudes cannot be changed by setting a numerical goal; hence leadership too is an old-fashioned concept for quality FM. You might get some grudging behavioral changes by imposing numerical goals, but it takes a leader to get people to embrace the attitudes that, for example, cause your service receptionist to totally focus on customers or make your custodial supervisor commit to continual improvement. The facility manager must set the tone. One of the things that you will learn over the years is how your employees (or your contract employees) are constantly assessing you. Are you fair? Are you tough? Are you a phony when it comes to quality? If you read Kouzes and Posner, two authors who write on leadership, they say that the most important thing for a leader is to be credible, and have a combination of honesty, competence, forward-vision and inspiration.[2] Almost anyone

The FM manager must set the tone.

A facility manager should be viewed as a leader throughout the company or agency.

One of the most important roles for the facility manager is to demonstrate by actions that quality is important.

Get an attitude!

can run a facility department in good times, but in times of stress or in times when attitudes must be changed, a leader is needed. We probably have written more on leading FM organizations than anyone else because we feel that the successful facility manager must not only lead his department but be a leader within the company or agency.

Here's one last point on a facility manager's attitude and leadership capabilities that we feel is especially important. One of your greatest roles as a manager of a quality FM organization is to create a climate that values, in fact expects, continuous improvement. We have been in organizations that valued constant improvement and in others, with equally good people, that suboptimized their resources because they tried to maintain the status quo. The latter, in fact, did not stay at the same level; they actually slipped backward and seemed to fear the objectives and challenges facing them. That attitude started at the top. This type of attitude in the FM department is particularly important in a company or agency where TQM is not being practiced throughout the organization. Your efforts at quality FM may not always fall on receptive ears, if your own top management hasn't fully embraced the quality concepts. If you want to institutionalize quality within your own organization, you will have to demonstrate through leadership qualities that continuous improvement is the way to go.

If you don't show that you value continuous improvement, then your department won't either. Even if you do, you must reinforce it continually by the incentives that you give and the disincentives that you use. Our experience has been that the use of incentives is much more important than punishment and that you must be prepared, in the final analysis, to rid your organization of a few individuals who simply refuse to "get the word."

Continuous improvement not only is one of the linchpins of quality FM, but is most important to the management implementation. The manager can best spend time understanding this concept and ensuring that the attitudes involved are held by all, down to the last designer, mail room clerk, switchboard operator, plumber, hammer swinger, and cafeteria worker. Unless all of them know that they are expected above all to be improving their work process continually, departmental improvement will be truly limited.

In other words, if you are to be a really successful leader as a facility manager, you too need to get an attitude. Having surveyed many FM organizations, it is really evident that, while resources are extremely important, those FM organizations that are truly successful are so because they have strong leadership and a will. To summarize our philosophy on leading and having an attitude, we share with you six attitudes which seem common to the really outstanding FM organizations:

Outstanding FM organizations share these six attitudes.

- They want to be the best (and really feel that they are, normally with good reason).
- They don't just want to please customers, they want to delight them.
- They are proactive to the point of being aggressive. They treat problems as challenges.
- They constantly want to improve.
- They view the facilities as theirs (at all levels; employees, consultants and contractors) and view themselves as facilities specialists rather than specialists in their narrow field.
- Everyone takes responsibility for facilities problems; there is no "buck passing."

Hopefully nothing we have said here leads you to believe that quantitative management is passé. That is not true. We use many numerical indicators, but know from sad personal experience that you never can rely solely on the numbers. Numbers can indicate problem areas that need to be checked out but, as we have learned over the years, to act on a number without getting, as Paul Harvey says, "the rest of the story," almost always is disastrous. You need to be a leader of your people and, through your actions as a leader, show your commitment to continuous quality improvement.

Don't forget about quantitative management, but remember Dr. Deming's statement about leadership.

ON THE MORE ANALYTICAL SIDE OF CONTINUOUS IMPROVEMENT

In Chapter Three we discussed the need to be willing to be measured, which is how we know whether or not we are improving. In order for you to manage a better department, your effectiveness should improve, your efficiency should increase, you should be more responsive and/or you need to improve your relevance. Hopefully, you will continue to improve in all four factors. Whether you are more responsive or more relevant will largely be determined by your customers and so, as we have said, they must be polled.

You also have to constantly evaluate your internal processes to determine where you can improve your effectiveness and efficiency. Fortunately for us, one easy way to improve process (or to look at process improvement) has been well-defined by the famous Shewhart cycle of Plan, Do, Check, and Act. As Figure 5.1 shows, this is an important concept whether you examine each component of the cycle, the cycle itself, or the cycle as a part of an ongoing, but continuously improving process. In this book, we have tried not to get tied to the form, bureaucracy, or mechanics of TQM, but in the Shewhart cycle, you see an easily understood concept that can systematize continuous improvement and produce results that are easily measurable. We like to think that the old-fashioned way is an orderly one and we believe that the Shewhart cycle is a simple, orderly way to look at continuous improvement.

Continuous improvement means plan, do, check and act!

FIGURE 5.1

THE SHEWHART CYCLE

Plan – Given a problem or simply a desire to improve, study your process. Try to establish where you are, who is involved, what data you have that is relevant, what possibilities exist for improvement and develop a plan.

Do – Try out the various possibilities for change according to, in your judgement, their likeliness of success. You must be committed to giving each improvement an honest effort and measuring impartially. You hedge your bet by experimenting generally on a small scale first.

Check – Measure the effect of your change against the baseline established in the planning stage. If not quantifiable, ask your customers, in some organized fashion, what they think of your change as opposed to your original process.

Act – If your change works, implement it. If not, try option two and repeat the cycle. If you want to further refine the process, start the cycle over again (Warning: any group of human beings can only accept so much change at one time. They can accept more change if they have been involved in the process of change.).

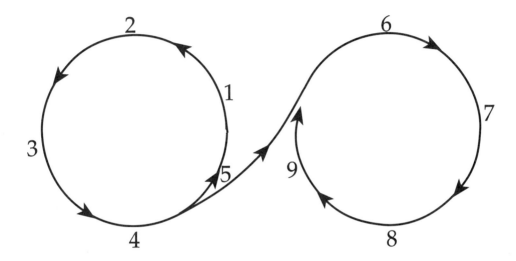

1. Plan;	4. Act;
2. Do;	5. Repeat with new information to try again, or;
3. Check;	6. Move to another process (6-9) with information gathered.

One last point before we move on. When you put on your analytical hat, we hope you won't take off your management one. When you introduce change, expect resistance. You can minimize it, and perhaps even co-opt the resisters, if you maximize their participation. Also, make the process just as "transparent" (open, honest, understandable) as you can. This is one of the reasons we find the Shewhart model helpful. You can understand it because it is simple and easily explained

If you maximize participation, you minimize resistance to change.

to others. Finally, make sure that no one is playing with either the measurements or the data. All things are not measurable, and your judgment and your team's judgment will be necessary continually, but the minute that there is a sensing that the "books are cooked" to support a particular change, your "goose will be cooked" also.

THE ORGANIZATION STRUCTURE ASPECTS OF CONTINUOUS IMPROVEMENT

Talking about organizational structure in the same breath as quality management usually rates right up there with the bubonic plague and housecleaning. Even two of our heroes in the quality movement, Tom Peters and Karl Albrecht, have been particularly anti-organizational structure. We think that is unfortunate, because a certain amount of structure is absolutely essential for good facility management. In fact, we feel that there must be a structure present that can take care of 95% of the requirements and problems without the intervention of the facility manager. The facility manager can then concentrate on that critical 5% of the problems that truly need his/her attention.

A Service Reception Center (SRC) can be the key to successful interaction with your customer for continuous improvement.

We are not going to focus on creating an organization structure for quality in this book, even though we think there is a definite trend to create FM organization structures which are driven by the customers (do you "smell" another book brewing?). We do want to spend a few minutes, however, talking about the importance of one organizational component, a Service Reception Center (SRC), to any FM organization structure. At any one location where FM services are provided, it is absolutely essential that work is received, prioritized, tasked, and coordinated centrally. Our terminology for that point is a Services Reception Center (SRC) but, whether it is the facility manager's secretary or a full-blown SRC, this organizational element is critical to quality FM.

There are several different philosophies about the proper role of the SRC. Our personal preference is for a highly automated SRC manned by personnel trained in telephonic customer service techniques. We are not concerned that they can solve the problems of the callers; we just want to assure that callers are directed to the proper place to get a solution, preferably without the need to redial. We envision the service receptionist, within guidelines, being able to type a service order directly into a system which sends hard copy to both a shop and back to the customer. The SRC also gathers data on frequency of complaints by category / trade and location / organization and tracks the response time for the SRC phone to be answered and also for the service order to be closed. In addition, it also is the hub where all facilities numbers and costs are generated for management and coordinated work so that a phone is not installed in a wall on Monday only to have the wall torn out as part of an alteration project on Wednesday. Many companies are using E-mail to task the facilities department directly or have a menu which can be called up to request facility services. We have included some examples of this concept in our Best Practices Chapter.

Our preference is for a more customer-oriented rather than technical SRC.

There is no right or wrong answer, but we emphasize the need for a central point that is knowledgeable about all of the department's activities and can provide centralized answers on costs, volume of work, response, etc. Finally, there is an additional benefit to an SRC which also is the downfall of many FM organizations. A good SRC allows you to speak to customers with one voice and one messenger. Within a large FM organization, coordination and good communications are very difficult, given all the functions. A properly run SRC can go far to solve those problems.

An SRC allows you to speak to your customer with one voice.

For those of you who still need additional reasons to be inspired about an SRC, we have them. First, in an SRC, one of the service receptionists or the supervisor, can be especially trained in customer service and can

Use an SRC for trouble spots.

handle the really difficult or obnoxious calls. This "trouble desk" concept can be a real bonus, if all receptionists are trained to quickly spot potential trouble or difficult customers and turn the caller over to the trouble desk quickly. If a caller feels he/she is just being passed from one nonresponsive person to another, you have lost more than you have gained.

Use an SRC to collect data.

Secondly, it can become the data center for gathering the good marketing information on customers we described in Chapter Four and for managing the sampling of customer attitudes through telemarketing, surveys or response cards we discussed in Chapter Three. Whatever form your SRC takes, our point here is that we feel an SRC is an excellent organization tool to demonstrate your commitment to continuous improvement.

POWER TO THE PEOPLE – EMPOWER YOUR FM STAFF!

Fourth Pillar of Quality: The front line service worker should have the flexibility to decide how to handle a situation.

From our perspective, one of the five pillars of quality which we talked about in our Introduction is that employees of the FM organization must be empowered, be held responsible for their actions and view themselves and their jobs within a broad context. In other words, the front line service worker, as well as the rest of the FM staff, should have the flexibility and be empowered to make decisions with the customer. Some real examples of lack of empowerment, and their negative effect on the perceptions of FM, help to illustrate our point.

- A customer who needed more light really was not very sympathetic to the light bulb replacement worker who went to the office and determined the bulb was okay, the problem was probably with the switch. Then the worker went on to another assignment;

- The handyman for an FM organization who visited a customer to replace a door knob, had to ask "management" if he could stay to tighten a screw on a chair;

- A print shop manager who needed a new machine hooked up was less than impressed when a plumber was sent without an electrician even though the customer only asked for a plumber; and

- The custodial staff who were in 99% of an organization's facilities every day, yet consistently failed to report deficiencies in those same facilities.

In situations like these, your FM staff need to have the flexibility and support from management to make decisions when they are interacting with their customers. If you are to rekindle the flame for pride in workmanship and build a quality ethic which has every FM employee taking responsibility for the facilities, then you need to create an environment which tells the staff that they are empowered to make decisions. You want each and every individual within your organization to be eager and willing to wear a button emblazoned with "IT'S MY JOB" on it to signify that they all feel empowered to make customer-based decisions.

This is how we rekindle pride in workmanship.

From situations like the ones above, we have come up with three simple rules that can serve as the basis for empowerment at the working level.

First – If you can fix something, do it then and do it right the first time;

Second – If health, safety or operations are involved, when you come upon a facility deficiency that you cannot fix, take responsibility for seeing that it is reported to the right person immediately and take the responsibility for following up to make certain it was fixed; and

Third – Fix anything you can see as you go through the facilities and if you can't fix it, report it to someone who can and take responsibility for following up with that person to make certain it was fixed.

Three simple rules for empowerment at the working level.

Implementation of this type of empowerment requires some training (which we will talk about next) and some procedures for workers to follow. First of all, the housekeeping staff, for example, must be able to determine how best to take care of the facilities. They need to determine if they want to do team cleaning, zone cleaning or whatever it takes to ensure that they

We do not advocate management without procedures.

know it is their job and they take pride in doing it. Second, we do not advocate management without procedures. You do not want the light bulb installer to be an electrician, if the worker is not trained to be one. Each worker must know what he or she should fix and what should be reported when in doubt. Again, we are advocating good, old-fashioned common sense. Third, people need to be given the time necessary to be "facility specialists" not just light bulb changers, custodians, electricians, etc. Initially, it may take longer to do work on an as needed basis than it does to respond to one call at a time, but the long-term benefits are far greater. Finally, you have to encourage this attitude and periodically reinforce the fact that you expect everyone to ferret out every facility deficiency or enthusiasm will peter out. It is just human nature.

If you still are not convinced that empowerment works, just enter into a discussion with your staff and some of your colleagues on the subject. It always is interesting to us to discuss empowerment with a group of workers, supervisors and managers, since you can almost predict the attitudes that will be expressed:

- Supervisors will look at empowerment as a direct attack on their performance and ability to control their work units;
- Managers will embrace the concept in the abstract but will not have the foggiest idea of what it really means to them in the implementation and will worry that they won't be needed to make decisions; and
- Workers will enthusiastically endorse it at first. After a bit of discussion, some will view it as just one more management attempt to get more work out of them without additional compensation.

Realistically, there is some truth to all of the opinions expressed above and some of the attitudes behind them. Yet, when all of the griping is over, for the most part you know that work is one of the most important things to most FM folks you know. You will have to admit that it is scary to think about some people who have worked with you in FM over the years and how dedicated they have been. We are certain you know of, as we both do, workers who sleep on a job site to make sure that you meet a deadline. You have heard of them driving two hours through a blizzard to make sure that a special job was completed on time. You also have lost count of the thousands of folks who have worked on weekends to make certain that a move was finished by opening of business on Monday morning. Then why is it, we wonder, so hard for you to believe in empowerment when you all know that for the most part people will do the right thing?

Why do we have problems with empowerment? Think of all your staff who have gone above and beyond the call of duty.

Those of you whose management careers have spanned the last few decades should realize that the workers of today, just like those you worked with in years past, want to be treated as individuals who have decision making capabilities. Successful empowerment allows you to capitalize on this desire by taking into account the importance that most people place on their work and the fact that we all are in a period where the nature of the work itself is in transition. People are ready and able to be empowered, if you provide the necessary skills.

THE ROLE OF TRAINING IN QUALITY FM

We probably share your frustration in that you al-ways seem to have to scramble for training funds. We have never really understood why that is, since we are the type of people who judge others and organizations by where they put their resources. We really don't think that most organizations truly are committed to training their staff and inevitably that viewpoint will cause them to fall into the ranks of second class. In many companies and agencies where the FM organization does not con-trol its training funds directly, we know how hard it is for facility managers to obtain the funds for their staff to attend seminars, annual conferences and certification courses, let alone funds for quality and customer ser-vice training.

We know how hard it is to obtain training funds, but customer service training is essential.

Our argument for this type of training goes to the very heart of quality FM, however. Just because you have created an environment in which the FM staff feel empowered to perform their jobs, it doesn't necessarily mean that they have the requisite skills to do so. Empowering your carpenters and movers does not automatically make them good customer representatives. Yet, if you empower them, you have to expect that they can, at a minimum, make a favorable customer contact and verify the service to be performed, perform the service, make a determination to provide a secondary service if one is required, get some customer feedback, be capable of properly disconnecting from a problem customer without a scene and use some quantitative tools and techniques for measuring the service delivery. This level of empowerment can only be accomplished by providing training in more nontechnical areas related to customer service.

Empowerment without training will not work.

We cannot stress strongly enough the value of providing customer service training for each and every individual within your FM organization. If you are skeptical about this level of commitment to training, think about something we routinely tell our clients about the importance of customer service training. In any FM organization, your customer service orientation on any given day is only as good as your worst performer that day. Why? Because that one poor performer may be a customer's only contact with the FM organization and that is how your customer will form a *perception* of how the total organization delivers its service. Sound familiar? Remember our discussion from Chapter One? Very few FM organizations can afford that kind of adverse publicity. You need every individual to be aware of what it takes to provide quality, customer-oriented service, if your whole organization is going to be successful.

Your FM organization is only as good as your worst performer on any given day.

Quality FM based on customers is a concept which has to be part of your continuous improvement strategy. Even the best FM organizations try to spend consistent, regular time on customer service problems and "brainstorming" ways to solve them. Your organization can't rest on its laurels if it is receiving high marks from its customers, because the minute the organization fails to focus on quality and customer service, it no longer is central to the fabric of the organization.

We do not want to appear prescriptive in our approach to training, but we do want to be helpful to those of you who may not know how to structure this type of training. Many facility managers feel comfortable with the more traditional technical training associated with the FM business and do not know how to go about developing a training curriculum which couples the skills necessary for empowered decision making with customer service. To guide you in these efforts we have developed a content outline for a one-day training session which includes skills building on empowerment and customer service.

You can't rest on your quality laurels — strive to improve.

FIGURE 5.2

TRAINING SESSION ON EMPOWERMENT AND CUSTOMER SERVICE

- Concept of self-directed work teams;
- Problem solving in a collaborative environment;
- Developing a customer service attitude;
- Understanding the customer drives the process;
- Measuring quality and customer service (tools and techniques);
- How to deal with angry customers;
- The importance of feedback on service to customers;
- The customer you can't see – the telephone customer;
- When to get your supervisor involved; and
- The importance of marketing FM services.

PARTNERING FOR QUALITY FM

Focusing on your customer, instilling pride of workmanship, empowering staff to make decisions and solve problems, and providing training are critical components of our recipe for continuous improvement. In our discussion thus far in this chapter we have been talking

FM organizations have a responsibility to partner with vendors for quality service delivery.

about continuous improvement as it applies to an in-house FM organization only. But what about FM services which more and more are being outsourced? What is your responsibility to ensure that quality is as important to your suppliers as it is to your own staff?

We feel it is the responsibility of the facility manager to drive the contracting process in such a way as to create a partnership with the potential vendors. Traditionally, most goods and services in large FM organizations have been purchased through competitive bidding. Under competitive bidding, most companies have the department desiring the goods or services prepare the technical specifications and then the purchasing department will attach a set of general conditions and some bidding instructions. The winning bidder normally is selected by a process that assures minimal technical competency but is primarily based on price. There are many variations and subtleties but the philosophy is to write the specifications correctly, then let the market decide which vendor will provide the good or service based on price.

There are several problems with this approach. First of all, it is highly dependent upon the quality of the specification. Since that is the part of the contracting package that the FM organization prepared, if there is a problem with the contractor, your tendency is to add more restrictions (and more volume) to the technical specs. How many of you have been told by your purchasing agent or contracting officer when a vendor was not performing as you wished, "Well, you wrote the specs?" We recently reviewed a specification for a custodial contract for a public agency that ran over 350 pages!

Huge specification packages are not the answer to problems with quality service.

One of the things you all have to realize is that you will never write the perfect specification or one that covers everything. Don't try! You and your purchasing department are putting your emphasis in the wrong area. When we write specifications, our entire document seldom exceeds 20 pages for our service contracts.

We emphasize expectations, relationships and the opportunities to mutually benefit from improvements rather than trying to spell out every technical situation that the contractor can expect to encounter when providing services in our facilities. We often have joked that the perfect technical service specification contains a paragraph describing the services desired and the second paragraph need only be, "Do it right the first time." In fact, we know some companies that go only a little beyond this statement in developing their Requests for Proposals (RFP's). You probably do not intend to continue a relationship with a firm which is going to "nickel and dime" you to death, so you need only to spell out your needs in a general way when writing specifications. Specs writing is not easy; you just concentrate on different, we think more important, issues.

Maybe we need a two-page spec which says, "Do it right the first time."

Before we get deeper into this topic, we have to caution that we neither want to usurp the authority of the purchasing departments, nor do we feel that the processes we advocate must apply to every procurement, but certainly they are important for the critical supplies and services purchases...those that affect your core functions. If your company is embracing quality "the old-fashioned way," the purchasing agents and contracting officers who serve you will view you as their customer and work with you to produce procurements which serve your needs best. FOR TOO LONG, THE PURCHASING DEPARTMENT, FORTRESSED BY COMPANY FEARS ABOUT GRAFT AND CORRUPTION, HAS PROMOTED PROCUREMENTS WHICH WERE NOT IN THE BEST INTEREST OF THEIR CUSTOMERS OR THE OVERALL GOOD OF THE COMPANY/AGENCY. We personally know of the following situation.

An incumbent contractor, whom all acknowledged was performing well, lost a contract by less than $13,000 on a $3,000,000 annual requirement merely because the procurement rules said that all contracts needed to be rebid after three years. The ironical twist to this story *is that the new contractor failed to perform and had to be terminated after less than a year. The old contractor was brought back in, but by this time, had sent all its experienced supervisors to other work sites. It took two to three years to get service levels back to where they were initially. In this instance, everyone lost by a procurement policy which could have been changed.*

All complicated procurement rules have succeeded in doing, in many cases, is to foster a "low-bid, let's see how we can make our money on change orders" mentality among your vendors. And when you give them a 350 page document to work on, we guarantee, they can find many loopholes to attack. While no one wants to talk about it (we call it the nasty little secret of procurement), many contracts are bid under cost with the contractor knowing full well that he/she will make a profit on change orders. In fact, constantly rebidding some of the services that you procure almost assures that profit margins are reduced to the point that the contractor cannot make a profit. That is unrealistic. If a contractor "buys in" he/she has to make a profit some way, by providing inferior service, underpaying staff or plaguing you with change orders. Everyone who is experienced in procurement knows this, yet we cling to outdated processes due to institutional inertia and the "bogey-man" of corruption. It took the Japanese, who have a societal bias in this direction, to teach us how to use vendors by having them "buy in" to the production of quality products and services within our companies and agencies.

Many private companies are experiencing a real revolution in their procurement procedures emphasizing simpler contracts and long-term relationships or partnering with vendors. Reinventing government promises this to the federal government as well, but whether the constant fear about empowering the technical experts in the procurement process will ever be overcome remains to be seen. Regardless of whether you are in the public or private sector, you can hasten this process by seeking management support, with the

The contractor has to "buy into" a commitment to quality with the client.

quality movement as your source, for reducing the number of your vendors and for establishing long-term relationships with those who work with you and constantly produce the goods and services which allow you to provide quality FM for your company or agency. These are some of the benefits of reducing the number of vendors and establishing long-term relationships:

Long-term relationships with outsourced firms are one way to partner for quality.

- The vendor can stabilize service and personnel, which is an advantage to both you and the vendor;
- The administrative costs of procurements (pure overhead) can be minimized;
- The vendor can afford to be more innovative when given the surety that an investment can be recovered over a longer period of time assured by a long-term contract;
- The vendor can be made to feel a part of "the team" rather that a "hired gun" and will have time to develop the relationships necessary for good teamwork. Interestingly, the employees who work for contractors with whom you have a long-term relationship actually develop a loyalty to your facilities team; and
- Particularly if your facilities are complex, you save the cost of constant reorientation of personnel due to the changing of contractors.

The reality of the situation is that your vendors perform better if they are included in the process from the beginning. We know of several companies that use potential vendors in the specifications development process to partner with the company up front. We advocate that you bring potential vendors into the decision making process before the RFP is written to take advantage of their wisdom from being in the business. If you follow this procedure you will ensure that at least some of the following issues get addressed before you begin contract negotiations:

Include your vendors in the process from the beginning.

- With partnering up front, you can address the time allowed for on-site training and who will provide or compensate for it;
- Either you or your contractor will have to provide

some language training, basic literacy training and customer service training. Our personal preference is that you can share the time for the former, but you develop your own site specific customer service program which should be required for everyone who might come in contact with employees of your company or agency. This way, you control how customer service is internalized for the vendor;

- Those contract staff now will represent you; their appearance, demeanor, competence and ability to blend in with the staff are all important issues to you. Your vendor should be transparent to your customers who should not be able to distinguish contract from in-house FM staff; and

- Another aspect of empowerment will be the need for multi-skill facility mechanics. A facility handyman should, for example, know how to balance a door, install a simple lock, patch carpet tile and change a washer in a faucet. Staffing limitations will place a high value on this type of tradesman and you will want to know how your contractor will handle the hiring of these folks.

As a profession, we are just learning how to write contract documents to meet these new demands, but it is clear that the old, thick technical specification is on its way out (Glory Be!), to be replaced with relatively thin contracts that define expectations and relationships between parties. As we find FM functions increasingly outsourced, good vendor relationships not only will be important, they will be critical. To take the point to the extreme, if all there is between you and your vendor is a two page document, you will never provide quality FM services. On the other hand, if you make your vendors feel they are partners with your organization and have a vested interest in working closely with you, then you and your contractor will know you are going to work collaboratively on problems and solutions over the long run.

Just as managers in other professions are doing, you should be judged on your "product," the FM services

You need to work collaboratively with your provider to solve problems.

that you render as prescribed and evaluated by your customers. A purchasing department should not be dictating, for your critical vendors, either which contractor you use or the cost of those services, as long as there is nothing illegal or immoral in your selection of those vendors. There is a new management world out there which is returning to tried and tested (old-fashioned by our definition) business practices and many facility managers need to help lead their purchasing departments into it. We need to place greater importance on the role of the customer in the procurement requirement process. If your company or agency does not have a quality management program which promotes reducing the number of vendors and establishing long-term partnerships, you will have to be an innovator and promote change in this area. If you don't no one else will.

The customer should be our primary consideration in the procurement requirement process.

AVOIDING THE "I HAVE ALWAYS DONE IT THIS WAY" SYNDROME

The need to constantly question your premise is one principle that seems particularly applicable to the FM business. It is closely tied to committing to continuous improvement. Those of you who have been in your positions for a long time, who have established top-flight organizations which perform well, can become complacent. As mentioned repetitively in this chapter, the world is changing. For example, the addition of a new product line in your company which requires the first ever clean room will dramatically change the way you practice FM. The same is true for the introduction of a process that produces hazardous waste which you must collect, store and dispose of. The regulatory climate of the 90's is much different than that of the early 80's and undoubtedly facility managers will have additional regulatory change to cope with even as we are still trying to adjust to the Americans with Disabilities Act (ADA). If you continue with the same policies, the same organization, the same standards and the

Don't get trapped by the "entrenched" way of doing things.

same procedures, you will find yourself not only out-of-date, but possibly in violation of the law. You need to constantly challenge the premise upon which you structured these policies and your organization.

In one way or another, all of you head some type of bureaucracy. It is inevitable that bureaucracy develops. In order to maintain yourself competitively, however, you need to periodically challenge your premise to include what services you are providing and how best to provide them. One of the positive outcomes of outsourcing studies is that, if you do them properly, they cause you to examine what you do and how you do it in a systematic manner. They allow you to avoid the trap of doing things the same way just because they have always been done that way. At the middle manager and worker level particularly, it is hard to sustain one program, even one that is based on continual improvement and, therefore, changing constantly. We all tend to turn our jobs into routines the longer we are in them. One of the real challenges then, is to keep things fresh. We have developed some techniques to help make sure you are fighting against corporate sclerosis and continuing to improve at the same time.

Some tips for avoiding FM organization sclerosis!

- Have a total review of at least one function annually. Zero base the budget at the same time;
- Change your review procedures. One year do it top down; another year bottom up. Include customers sometime in your reviews;
- Stress responsiveness for a time. Then stress efficiency/cost effectiveness; and
- Use different techniques to sample your customers' response: surveys, response cards, telephone surveys, focus groups, etc.

Vary your own approach too.

If you do not vary your approach, the law of diminishing returns will undoubtedly start to take hold. For example, our return rate on customer-completed project surveys went from 70% to 30% to 10% in successive years. Our staff did not read the service order history reports as carefully after about six months. You too lose your interest in aspects of quality management the more familiar that you are with them. Therefore your staff loses interest BECAUSE THE STAFF ALWAYS DOES BEST WHAT THE BOSS CHECKS. Quality management gives you all sorts of metrics and techniques. Use them all but, as the Shewhart Cycle tells you, work new metrics into your tools and continue to plan, do, check and act.

ONE MORE LOOK AT THE BIG PICTURE – STAY FOCUSED ON THE FUTURE

We have talked thus far about leadership, empowerment, training and attitude in this chapter and are just about ready to move on to those practices that have made our colleagues successful. Before we do, we would like to summarize our concept of continuous improvement. From our perspective, continuous improvement must start by measuring the perception of your customers. Do they see you improving? How do you know? You must use all the tools and techniques we have discussed throughout the book to make this customer connection. The corollary to continuous improvement is continuous feedback. As we have mentioned many times, tap into your customers at every level and then have techniques to get that information to you. You personally have to talk to your colleagues and above in the company because only you can tap that level. Even if there were no quality efforts, an organization and its services would deteriorate unless effectiveness, efficiency and responsiveness were constantly being upgraded. Time grinds heavily and finely on the FM organization that stays static and you as the FM leader must be committed to continuous improvement and ensure that each and every member of your staff is as well. Too many professional facility managers lead their lives so bound up in the present, they fail to provide for their future. We have included some tips we think will help you to stay focused on your future:

You must look beyond today, and today's problems and issues. Provide for the future.

- Know the business you support, the language of business (ratio analysis, net present value analysis/

internal rate of return (IRR), depreciation calculation, etc.), and how to show that your department supports the company/agency;

- Be better about internal and external relations. Promote and market your organization;

- Really listen to your customers and remember they and they alone define your services and how you perform them;

- Become a better communicator by improving both your business writing and oral presentation skills;

- Read professionally, particularly business periodicals and management and leadership journals;

- Be a futurist by staying tuned in to the current issues in the FM profession. The Association of Higher Education Facilities Officials (APPA), The American Institute of Plant Engineers (AIPE), BOMA and IFMA can help here as they continually run training on cutting-edge issues;

- Constantly talk to vendors about new products and services. You want to know what the competition has to offer as well as what you might want to purchase. Many of them actually will give you a "sneak preview" of their developmental items if you are a good enough customer;

- Stay abreast of the emerging legal and regulatory issues which seem to be just exploding in our profession. The professional and trade associations can help here; and

- Improve your analytical skills, particularly those which allow you analyze your efficiency, effectiveness, responsiveness, and your customer's evaluations of your services.

The major reward will be in serving your customers better.

You need to pursue continuous improvement in your professional lives to no less an extent than you see continuous improvement in your FM organization. Where you will see the major rewards will be in serving your customers better. We wish you continued luck in the great FM journey. To let you know that others have traveled down the path to quality FM, in our next chapter we will examine some of the practices that successful facility managers recommend for continuous improvement.

END NOTES

1. W. Edward Deming, *Out of the Crisis* (Cambridge, MA: Massachusetts Institute of Technology Center for Advanced Engineering Study, 1986), p. 72.

2. James M. Kouzes and Barry Z. Posner, "The Credibility Factor: What Followers Expect from Their Leaders," *Management Review* , January 1990, pp. 29-33.

CHAPTER 6

THE QUALITY
MANAGEMENT WAY:
BEST PRACTICES

As we stated in our forward, a primary mission of this book is to showcase the quality management efforts of our colleagues. Our strategy was to use the "Best Practices" idea initiated by the IFMA Focus Group. We did not want lengthy case studies, but rather concise, practical examples of what facility managers have been able to accomplish with respect to quality management.

In the fall of 1993, we issued a call for quality management Best Practices. The response was overwhelming and only served to reinforce what we already knew — facility managers everywhere have been quality leaders. We wish to thank all of you for your generous contribution to our endeavor. It was difficult trying to decide which Best Practices to include. Clearly we could have produced a lengthy book based solely on the accomplishments of others. In truth, we may decide to use the idea as a sequel to this book.

For this book, however, we have included Best Practices which we feel are a diverse, yet representative sample of quality FM efforts. The contributors have graciously agreed to include their names and telephone numbers to make it easier for you to contact them. We know you will find their Best Practices helpful and encourage you to network with them.

BEST PRACTICE

TITLE:

Contracting Team Structure

CONTACT:
Mr. Barry Yach
Section Manager, Property Management
Bell Canada
Main Plaza, 160 Elgin Street
Ottawa, ONT K1G 3J4

613-781-5384

SUMMARY:

The Property Management division of Bell Canada, Ottawa, Ontario is developing a new way of doing business. Driven by the desire to be cost competitive, quality and customer focused, the Property Management's typical hierarchical organization structure is being transformed into a project driven contractor-type of structure.

BENEFITS:

This provides opportunities for teamwork, employee development and cost efficiencies comparable to market competition. This initiative involves a team of 35 people responsible for 2.0 million square feet in Eastern Ontario. This initiative will reduce operating costs by $850.0 k in 1993 on a base of $4,000 k.

Traditional Organization
- Based on geographical territory, i.e., span of control "1 coach per 8 technicians"; and
- Coach and technicians dedicated to specific locations and job functions.

New Organization

- Project driven with defined costs, start and finish milestones;
- Structured like a contracting business, i.e. span of control "1 coach per 25-35 technicians"; and
- Technicians empowered through training and coaching.

Introduction of this team concept will:

- Reduce labor cost by $850.0 k in 1993;
- Maximize the efficiency of resources;
- Develop a breakthrough strategy to meet business plan objectives;
- Promote and create opportunities for employee development; and
- Build on the team concept and learning from team projects.

Built with volunteers.

Project oriented approach to work.

Distinctive name chosen for this team was Bell Realty Services (BRS) Contracting to symbolize new mindset.

In-depth communication plan developed and implemented.

Mode of Operation

- The teams are being given the control, responsibility, appropriate training and accountability to operate without direct supervision;
- Weekly meetings are held with the teams to identify areas of concern and/or problems;
- All jobs and work assignments are assigned in the form of a project, i.e. with an agreed upon start and stop time;
- Gradual process;
- Communication plan is very important, i.e. unions, customers, internal;
- Must establish a leader within each group (not a

coach); a person with the right mindset and philosophy to lead each group;

- Teams are physically removed from the traditional business operation;
- Must set up an accounting and tracking system for all teams (groups) to measure efficiency; and
- The teams are responsible for interfacing directly with the Control Centers and BRS office, i.e. safety check-in, service orders, receiving and returning work orders, scheduling time off, etc.

TRAINING REQUIREMENTS

- Safety;
- Driving reviews;
- Customer focus;
- PR training;
- Ongoing training required in new technical and interpersonal skill set areas;
- Team building training;
- Tools; and
- Vehicles.

BUILDING OWNERSHIP

People are assigned building locations for which they are primarily responsible, i.e., responsible for overall inspections and overall knowledge. "Personal Building Ownership" includes being responsible for reporting on the conditions of:

- Roofs;
- Control systems;
- General maintenance;
- HVAC conditions;
- Life support systems; and
- Cleaning conditions.

Bell Canada - Property Management

BRS Team for Ottawa Metro area...

BRS Contracting Team Structure

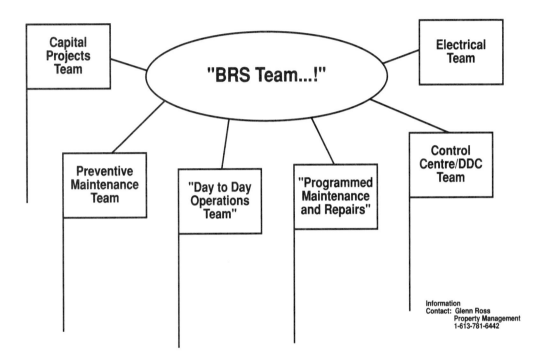

Information
Contact: Glenn Ross
Property Management
1-613-781-6442

BEST PRACTICE

TITLE:

Group Self Assessment: A Tool for TQM Success

CONTACT:

Frank Yockey
Quality/Productivity Manager
Hewlett-Packard
3404 E. Harmony Road
Fort Collins, CO 80525

303-220-2140

SUMMARY:

Many quality programs in the U.S. are not meeting expectations for improved performance. The concerns vary broadly from lack of measurability of progress in quality achievement to impact on the bottom line. In fact, some critics suggest that the whole quality movement has been a distraction to U.S. industries' ability to make significant productivity improvements in the past decade. Unfortunately, many companies have backed away from their quality efforts. Employees are frustrated and managers already are giving up on their quality programs. Much of the problem is a result of lack of measurability of progress and identification of issues for focused improvement.

Assessment methods such as the Baldrige criteria can be helpful, but they can also be difficult to administer and usually do not give timely and useful feedback to the first level employees. The concept of a group self assessment, based on a Baldrige or similar criteri,a can be effectively administered right down to the worker level. Self assessments can effectively institutionalize quality, focus efforts on the critical few improvement areas, and drive learning in the organization. Self assessments can quickly increase productivity.

Self reviews can be adapted to a wide range of quality programs. Two such implementations and the positive effects upon the organization are discussed.

Hewlett Packard's Total Quality Control (TQC) awareness heightened significantly following HP's Japanese subsidiary winning the Deming Prize in 1982. A great deal was learned from this endeavor in terms of what it would take to really transform HP into a true quality driven company. The TQC program was christened as a global HP management philosophy at a World Wide Quality Managers Meeting in 1983. The goal of this effort was to institutionalize the program throughout the company in five years.

BENEFITS:

- Improved quality maturity of the organization;
- Improved effectiveness and productivity from the organization; and
- Improved customer satisfaction.

MEASUREMENTS:

Each of the processes has specific measurements associated with the reviews.

SUCCESSFUL REVIEW INGREDIENTS

Some of the ingredients for a successful review include the need for open and honest discussions. There is no room for hidden agendas and politics. A good reviewer will quickly surface key issues. Participants need to be willing to learn and share ideas, thoughts and judgements openly. This means moving from the idea of audits being pass/fail adversarial relationships to an open environment where everyone can discuss the possibilities and arrive at the best solution for the organization. People need to show actual work. No new slides are permitted to be generated for the review. It has been difficult to get people to minimize preparation for a "dog and pony" show. The emphasis is on short presentations and lots of dialogue.

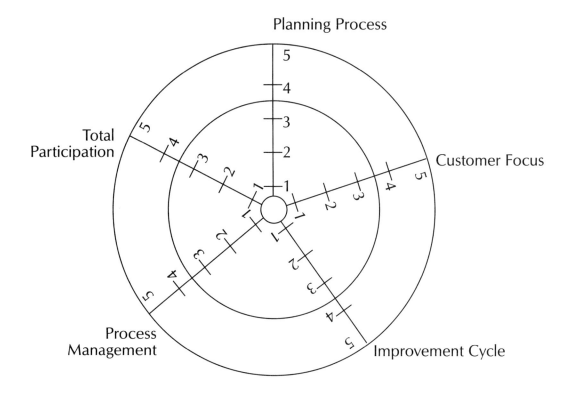

QUALITY MATURITY SYSTEM (QMS) DIMENSIONS

Shown above are the five dimensions of quality for HP's QMS program. Below, each of the elements is listed with a brief description of the focus and key areas of interest.

Planning Process
- Focus:
    - Review the entity planning process – long range to annual;
    - Has it improved over time?; and
    - How are key issues selected?
- Key areas of interest:
    - "Planning Wheel" process for strategic and annual plans;
    - Use of vision or purpose and direction to set entity direction;

- Annual plan linkages to long-range plans and to previous annual plans/results;
- Key issue selection process; and
- Plan linkage to product/service strategy.

Customer Focus

- Focus:
  - Approach used to understand customer needs; and
  - Approach used to measure and improve customer satisfaction and competitiveness.
- Key areas of interest:
  - Knowledge and stratification of customers and their needs;
  - Integration and use of customer data for product definition, satisfaction, etc.; and
  - Knowledge and use of competitors' data.

Improvement Cycle

- Focus:
  - Review efforts to improve products and services. Includes projects tied to Hoshin breakthrough objectives and business fundamental improvement.
- Key areas of interest:
  - Linkage of improvement projects to annual plans;
  - Use of logical and systematic problem solving approach;
  - Use of data; and
  - Documentation and methods for sharing lessons learned and standardization.

Process Management

- Focus:
  - Review the management of the division's key processes.
- Key areas of interest:
  - Identification and documentation of key processes;
  - Monitoring (with metrics) of key processes and the control of deviations; and

– Continuous improvement of key processes.

Total Participation

• Focus:
  – Leadership of quality efforts
  – How quality improvement efforts are directed, funded and tracked; and
  – Provisions for capturing individual suggestions and rewarding these efforts.

• Key areas of interest:
  – How are the entity visions communicated, reinforced;
  – Process to charter quality improvement teams and select issues to be addressed;
  – System for monitoring progress;
  – Type of training given; and
  – Process for capturing, evaluating, and rewarding suggestions.

THREE DIMENSIONS OF ASSESSMENT

Each of the elements is reviewed along three different dimensions shown below. This gives the management team a complete picture of how their maturity is progressing. There are a variety of ways the scoring can be done; there is no one "right" way. This is largely up to the discretion of the review team and their preferences.

Approach: Use of quality management tools, techniques and methods in the entity's business practices.

Development: The extent to which approaches are applied to all areas and activities within the entity's business.

Results: The outcomes and effects in achieving the purposes addressed and implied in the review categories and questions.

DURATION:

The QMS reviews were started in November, 1992 and are continuing to this date.

BEST PRACTICE

TITLE:

CLEANING QUALITY MANAGEMENT

CONTACT:

Dan Nordmark
Facilities Manager
Boeing Defense & Space Group
499 Boeing Boulevard, Mail Stop JW-50
Huntsville, Alabama 35824-6403

205-461-3921

SUMMARY:

- Provide levels of cleaning to match customers' requirements, not "standards";
- Provide incentives for the cleaning crew to excel; and
- Involve customers in the inspection process.

BENEFITS:

A happier customer at reduced cost of operations.

LIMITS:

Limited number of firms willing to bid on cost plus incentive contracts.

MEASUREMENTS:

- Improvement in inspection report;
- Fewer callbacks;
- Lower turnover of personnel; and
- Lower bids; lower overall cost.

DURATION:

Continuous since May, 1992.

Cleaning Quality Management

The Cleaning Quality Management contract concept has replaced the standard task-frequency contract for janitorial services.

Scopes of work that included tasks such as vacuum offices daily, mop tiled floors weekly, or strip and wax tiled floors semi-annually have many times left the customer not satisfied even though the contract requirements have been met. The customer is really not satisfied with the contract itself. Unfortunately, defined tasks and frequencies for those tasks does not ensure cleanliness or customer satisfaction. Heavy traffic areas that may require tasks to be performed more frequently become extra cost. Extremely light traffic areas may not require the minimum contract tasks to be performed and become wasted cost.

The purpose of janitorial services is to provide a clean comfortable work environment for our customers. Cleanliness also extends product life of furniture, carpet and buildings.

Customer Involvement

The first step to implementing a quality concept contract is to enable the customers to assist setting targets and priorities. Customer input is gathered from random interviews and questionnaires. Finding out what is important to the customer at the beginning of the contract will help in achieving customer satisfaction later into the contract.

Continual customer feedback is solicited throughout the contract through focal group meetings, surveys and interviews. Maintaining customer satisfaction is a primary goal for the success of the quality concept contract.

Employee Ownership

Just as important as the customer role in this concept is the employee. Often employee turnover is high in these types of contracts. High turnover creates added costs of training new employees as well as work not accomplished. In this process, assigning ownership to the employee is essential. Because employees are responsible for specific areas and their targets are zero defects, the quality of their work may be measured. Cleanliness levels for employee zones are determined based on quality control inspections. Employees receiving cleanliness levels above the contract target may be eligible for awards or incentives.

QUALITY INSPECTIONS

Quality inspections are conducted by contract supervision, supplier supervision and whenever possible, the employee responsible for the area. Inspections are performed in random areas at routine intervals. The process counts the number of item defects from the total number of items inspected. Zero defects = 100% cleanliness level. Various items are inspected such as chairs, desks, carpet, telephones, file cabinets, etc. Specific defects are defined. For example, the chair is not just labeled as dirty or not acceptable, but the defect defined...the chair has dust on the back and arms. Explaining the specific defect allows for specific plans to correct the defect.

Monthly review meetings including the supplier supervision, the contract supervision and management are held to review the inspection reports. The inspection report provides performance trends for each employee, building cleanliness levels and identifies the top five cleaning defects. These reports are used in continuous quality improvement efforts to provide better service and to correct problem areas. The review team also identifies problem areas, recognizes top performers and incorporates customer feedback into the targets and priorities.

As targets are reached and surpassed by the supplier, the buildings become cleaner. Targets may be adjusted when needed. Cost may be renegotiated because, if at the beginning of the contract the cleanliness level is determined to be 40%, the labor and effort to reach an acceptable level of 75% is greater than if the building is rated at 70%. It becomes easier for the supplier to provide a better quality service.

LIMITATIONS

There may be a limited number of suppliers willing to commit by contract to maintain an acceptable cleaning level rather than how many times the floors will be vacuumed. The better the bid package is prepared and the concept is explained, the better bids the supplier will provide. Floor plans detailing exact room layouts, floor types and dimensions are important tools to the supplier. Defined targets and priorities should be determined and supplied in the bid package.

QUALITY CONSULTANTS AND AUTOMATED SYSTEMS

To ensure a fair rating of the cleanliness level of the buildings, a quality concept consultant (third party) is recommended when changing from the old task frequency type contract to the new quality concept. While using a third party consultant, training is provided to contract supervisions, as well as supplier supervision.

Using automated inspection systems allows for the actual inspections to be performed and the information reports are generated by the system. Information is stored in the computer so comparisons and trends are readily made. A printed inspection form of each area inspected is made and provided to the supplier supervisor. Employees are made aware of each problem found in their area so that they are able to correct the problem immediately.

BEST PRACTICE

TITLE:

Real Estate Breakthrough Goals Identification, Measurement and Continuous Improvement

- No real estate caused outages in data centers and key switching centers;
- Achieve "world-class" occupancy cost;
- Order of magnitude reduction in annual lease expenses;
- Achieve "world-class gross square footage (GSF)/ employee"; and
- Reduce energy consumption by 10% from 1992 levels.

CONTACT:

Thomas F. Doherty
Manager, Strategic Planning
Bell Atlantic Network Services Incorporated
Two Bell Atlantic Plaza
1320 North Court House Road
Arlington, VA 22201

703-974-5326

SUMMARY:

Creating Real Estate/Facilities Breakthrough Goals aligns the team to the corporation's key strategies and prioritizes work on our "Blue-Chip" processes. These goals promote the application of the Bell Atlantic Way (TQM) behaviors while radically improving Bell Atlantic's Occupancy Cost. The process was created within the department after detailed definition, consensus and communication. The goals were communicated at all levels which included the Office of the Chairman and each business unit President.

BENEFITS:

Order of magnitude occupancy cost savings have been identified and realized. The process has focused the efforts of all Real Estate Teams. The data is used as a vehicle to concisely communicate Real Estate/Facilities strategies at all levels. Requires commitment by the Real Estate Team to stretch beyond what is readily achievable. BA expects to radically improve real estate asset management efficiency by reducing the over-provisioning of space (GSF).

LIMITS:

- Reflects only large process output requirements, bottom-up process improvement required to improve performance;
- Data not readily available, data acquisition processes need to be defined;
- PC based data only the fix; "real time" data not yet available to field; and
- Requires careful definition in order to prevent dysfunctional behaviors.

MEASUREMENTS:

PROCESS:

Uploading of all BA Occupancy Cost information from numerous data sources: Real Estate Management Information System, Human Resources headcount data, Leasing/Planning information into Windows-Excel spreadsheets. Quarterly updating with Field Managers, update of Harvard Graphics charts distributed to field. Visible posters evident at each Team work location. Measurement results discussed at each Departmental Staff Meeting.

METRICS AND GOALS: SEE ABOVE RESPECTIVELY:

• Number of outages	Zero defects
• Occupancy cost and O.C./GSF	Benchmark
• Leased GSF and 1992 expenses	1977 goal

- GSF/employee   250 GSF/employee
                                        and PONC

- BTU consumption   10% reduction by
  and BER   1977

DURATION:

This process has been in place since 2nd quarter 1992. This process is linked to the planning cycle and is expected to continue up to the 1997 plan year.

©1993, Bell Atlantic, Network Services Group.

BEST PRACTICE

TITLE:

"FAC" – Facilities Request System

CONTACT:

Jaan Meri
Manager, Facilities Engineering and Operations
Celestica Inc.
844 Don Mills Road, 28/421
North York, Ontario

416-448-4517

SUMMARY:

   Electronic Facilities Request System for work to be done. All site personnel have access to a terminal and can generate a request to get Facilities work done. (See "FAC" screen). The system automatically: generates a request number; the date and time that the request was sent; ensures that the on-line request is sent with all of the required information (there are mandatory fields); and sends a note back to the requester informing him/her that the request has been received. A system matrix routes the request directly to the person responsible for doing the work.

BENEFITS:

   Increased cycle time is the major benefit. The request can be in the hands of the person who has to carry out the work in a matter of seconds. Also requests are not lost or delayed in internal mail. The mandatory fields on the "FAC" screen assist in getting better information from the requester, allowing the maintenance person to complete his/her work without having to get in touch with the requester. Increased cycle time has reduced the time required to respond and complete Demand Maintenance requests and thus improve customer service.

LIMITS:

Software written by Facilities group. Designed to be used on IBM's OV/VM system.

MEASUREMENTS:

Cycle time for Unscheduled Maintenance (USM) requests is the average time taken to complete all of the USM's for one month. The clock runs for 24 hours a day, five days a week. USM cycle time begins when a person pushes the PF key on the keyboard to send a "FAC" request. The cycle ends when the contractor leaves a tent card on the person's desk. In a 330,000 KGOSF office building, average monthly cycle times of 4.5 hours have been achieved on a consistent basis.

DURATION:

Program installed since 1990.

FACILITIES REQUEST SYSTEM ('FAC')

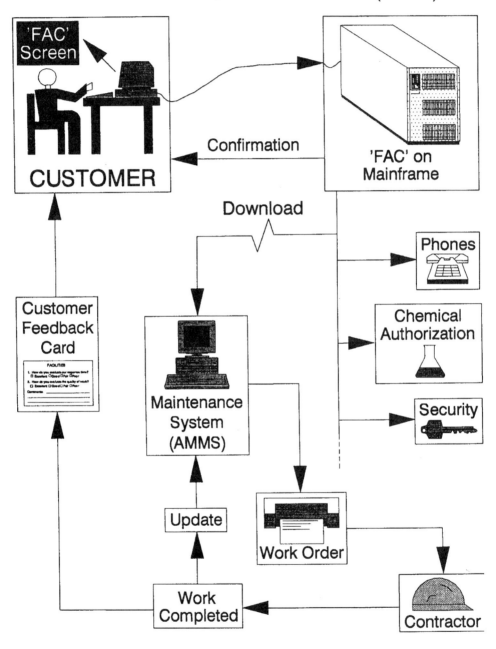

'FAC'Screen

```
10 Feb 1994                FACILITIES REQUEST SYSTEM

     Type selection number.  Then press ENTER.

—    1.   Safety  Exposures                        13.   Terminal  Support
     2.   Repairs  (Bldg,Furniture)                14.   Cafeteria  and  Catering
     3.   Temperature/Air  Quality                 15.   TBD
     4.   Rearrangement/Construction               16.   TBD
     5.   Workstation  Setup/Furniture             17.   TBD
     6.   People and Furn. Relocations             18.   TBD
     7.   Telephones  and  Phonemail               19.   Chemical  Authorization
     8.   Security/Keys/Locks/Passes               20.   Environmental  Impact  Assessment
     9.   Cleaning/Waste                           21.   Equipment  Data  Sheets
    10.   Name  Plates  and  Signs                 22.   Customer  Feedback
    11.   Cabling                                  23.   Search  (Facilities  use  only)
    12.   Other  Requests                          24.   Approve  a  Request


PF1   HELP          PF2   CONTACTS        PF3   QUIT        PF12   Return
```

BEST PRACTICE

TITLE:

Customer Feedback Card

CONTACT:

Jaan Meri
Manager, Facilities Engineering and Operations
Celestica Inc.
844 Don Mills Road, 28/421
North York, Ontario

416-448-4517

SUMMARY:

A Customer Feedback Card was developed to determine the effectiveness of the Demand Maintenance process. It asks the question, "Were you delighted?" Inside the card, the customer can express his or her opinion regarding response time and quality of work by selecting one of four answers: excellent, good, fair or poor. Only an "Excellent" response is counted. If a person answers "Good," he or she is not counted among the delighted. All "Poor" and "Fair" responses are investigated to determine the cause of dissatisfaction and to apply corrective action.

BENEFITS:

The card's most important benefit is the immediate feedback it provides on demand maintenance. It also instills ownership in the contractor who is doing the work and reinforces the message of customer service to the individual. It also informs the requester that the work has been completed.

LIMITS:

None. Easy and quick to implement.

MEASUREMENTS:

Delighted customers: 90% has been achieved (monthly measurement). Goal is 100%.

DURATION:

Ongoing since January 1991.

Printed on recycled paper.

Return to
28/421/844/TOR

FACILITIES SERVICES

Were you delighted???

☐	**B.G.**	
☐	**844**	***FACILITIES***
☐	**895**	
☐	**1150**	**Date:** _____

To improve our customer service, we would appreciate a few moments of your time to answer the following:

1. How do you evaluate our response time?
  ☐ Excellent   ☐ Good   ☐ Fair   ☐ Poor

2. How do you evaluate the quality of work?
  ☐ Excellent   ☐ Good   ☐ Fair   ☐ Poor

3. Type of work: _____

Comments / Suggestions: _____
_____
_____
_____

Name: _____ ***Ext.:*** _____

BEST PRACTICE

TITLE:

STAFF PRODUCTIVITY IMPROVEMENTS IN A TOTAL QUALITY ENVIRONMENT

CONTACT:

Mr. James E. Loesch, P.E.
Chief Facilities Engineer
Johns Hopkins University Applied Physics Laboratory
Building 25, Room 212
11100 Johns Hopkins Road
Laurel, MD 20723-6099

410-792-5134

SUMMARY:

The Plant Engineering Branch consists of 135 trades people providing new construction, renovation and refurbishment, and maintenance services for the 1.5 million square-foot facility. In 1992, their payroll exceeded $6.5 million.

Changing the hours of work, reducing the improper use of sick leave, and cutting down on break and lunch time has significantly improved the productivity of the Branch work force. These improvements were achieved through a combination of involving and educating staff, setting consistent policies within the Branch, and obtaining permission to change group work schedules while providing coverage during "normal" Laboratory operating hours.

Historically, the Plant Engineering work day included two fifteen minute breaks, taken in the shop break rooms, and a 1-hour lunch. When the Branch work hours were changed to 7:00 AM to 3:30 PM, the practice of taking breaks in a central location was eliminated at the suggestion of the Working Leaders (foremen). Also, a 30-minute lunch period was implemented which is consistent with the lunch period of other Laboratory employees.

BENEFITS:

As part of the ongoing Quality process, the Plant Engineering Branch surveyed its workers and discovered that 94% of the trades staff preferred to start and end their work day earlier than the professional staff. They like not having to work late in the hot summer and enjoy having more time off in the afternoons. Further, because the work day now starts one and a half hours before the Laboratory's normal starting time, many jobs that previously required overtime to avoid noise or disruption in the hallways, can now be done early in the morning on straight time. Clearly a win-win situation!

Line supervisors recognized that reducing the improper use of sick leave and tightening up on lunch and break times was necessary if the Branch was to continue to deliver a quality product cost-effectively.

LIMITS:

Changing the normal working hours for most of the Branch staff required a change in Laboratory policy. The means to provide trade coverage for the time between 3:30 PM and 5:00 PM also had to be worked out.

Of course, staff productivity improvement obtained through policy changes, although substantial, can be limited by the actions of each individual worker. To make long-term, sustainable improvements requires worker buy-in. Relating to workers as customers and partners has resulted in a sustained increase in productivity.

MEASUREMENTS:

- The average sick leave days used per nonexempt staff member in 1992 was reduced 1.7 days from the 1991 average for a savings of 1,300 man-hours.

- Starting the work day one and a half hours before the Laboratory's normal starting time has saved over 5,000 overtime hours per year.

- Changing the break and lunch time procedures has saved a minimum of 1 hour per day per person. Based on 1992 staffing levels, productive time was increased by 33,300 hours.

- The Plant Engineering Branch is continuing to monitor performance and has impaneled several Process Action Teams to explore other avenues to increased productivity.

- The combined effect of these three changes in 1992 resulted in a direct labor savings of almost $900,000.

DURATION:

These schedule and work habit changes were implemented in 1992 and are expected to continue indefinitely. The group has also experimented with other work schedules in certain areas, including a work week of four, 10-hour days and a work week shifted to include weekend days as part of the regular week.

BEST PRACTICE

TITLE:

The Infrastructure Planning Team (IPT) Process using the Facility Infrastructure Master Matrix (FIMM) tool

CONTACT:

Linda L. Flaherty
Engineering Planning Specialist
Lockheed Missiles & Space Company, Inc. (LMSC)
Orgn. 45-11/B509
1111 Lockheed Way
Sunnyvale, CA 94089-3504

408-524-6381

SUMMARY:

The Infrastructure Planning Team (IPT) is a multi-disciplined, cross-functional group of individuals with various facility operations responsibilities and technical expertise dealing with the basic facilities, equipment and installations needed for the functioning of a building or campus system. In a team setting, facility engineers (architectural, civil, structural, electrical, mechanical, etc.) collaborate with their counterparts in the maintenance and client organizations to identify and prioritize essential infrastructure projects based on age, condition of equipment, past service history and critical need of the system. Projects might be generated by changes in building and/or engineering codes, government regulations, statutes, ordinances and commitments and/or long-term repair and upgrade programs.

The identified infrastructure items are then input into the Facility Infrastructure Master Matrix (FIMM), a shared database tool, to perform strategic planning of basic facility requirements. The FIMM includes electrical, mechanical and structural systems, paved surfaces, utility systems and roofs, site master plan and other civil site facilities, emergency systems and energy conservation systems, maintenance, painting, and fire protection and safety related systems. Using the FIMM, projects are then prioritized to develop a 5-year and 10-year plan.

BENEFITS:

The team process allows for consensus decision making to prioritize infrastructure projects. The FIMM tool allows the long-range forecast of basic facilities requirements to be sorted by building, plant, type of work, risk management priority, funding category and budget year. The reports are made available to assist in the programming of customer driven projects. If extensive renovation to an area is necessary due to customer needs, then forecasted infrastructure projects can be integrated into the project to reduce and/or eliminate repeated disruption of an area. Projects mandatory by regulation (ADA, ozone-depletion, code interpretations) are given the highest priority and high visibility.

The process has assisted the facilities organization in getting the most out of available resources to keep the "City" of LMSC operating efficiently.

LIMITS:

The IPT process could be limited by the size and breadth of the facilities organization. It is best suited for a large corporation with campus-like building sites. A sufficient in-house staff of facility engineers and maintenance analysts require experience in performing condition assessments of infrastructure equipment and systems. A maintenance management system needs to be in place to track equipment service history.

The FIMM database was developed on Foxbase software for a Macintosh computer network. To develop this database for another company would require a dedicated computer programmer for 6-8 months, the purchase of a file server-oriented database software product, and an employee allocated to input and maintain data.

MEASUREMENTS:

The impact of this process on facilities management is measured by the approved budget levels of fixed assets for infrastructure projects and the percent of infrastructure projects to the total fixed asset budget.

DURATION:

The FIMM tool has been in place since 1990 and is constantly being modified. The IPT process was put into place in early 1991 and is undergoing continuous improvement to assure the highest quality of asset management.

BEST PRACTICE

TITLE:

TOTAL QUALITY MANAGEMENT PROCEDURES

CONTACT:

Mr. Charles Collins
Regional Manager
Landis & Gyr Powers, Inc.
1000 Deerfield Parkway
Buffalo Grove, IL 60089

708-215-1000

SUMMARY:

As facility managers, Total Quality Management (TQM) is a term you hear every day. It has most likely been adopted in some form by your organization as a program of high priority. However, the key to making TQM work is to treat it as a change in culture, not just a program.

TQM at Landis & Gyr Powers is becoming part of the culture, but not without commitment at all levels. Shortly after introducing the TQM concept to the company's facility managers, it became apparent that the cultural changes necessary at the maintenance personnel level would not come easily. As with most programs or concepts introduced by management, early perceptions were "it's just another program which will go away over time." Clearly, some early wins and demonstrated successes were necessary if management was to get the support of maintenance personnel.

With the aid of facility managers throughout the U.S. and Canada, Landis & Gyr Powers introduced a simple work request audit process to identify hurdles and road blocks in their service delivery. The audit reviews all activity, from the time the maintenance request is received through completion of the job and follow-up with the requester. The audit is done through a random sampling of work orders and is conducted by working supervisors and maintenance personnel.

BENEFITS:

The process allows management to quickly identify problem areas in the delivery of maintenance services. After reviewing the audit data they also use the computerized maintenance management system to identify the most frequently reoccurring maintenance requests. The findings are then presented to the maintenance personnel, and their suggestions on improving the process and reducing cycle time are solicited.

LIMITS:

None

MEASUREMENTS:

At each site Landis & Gry Powers has been able to identify and correct several processes which improved the maintenance services provided to their internal customers. They have been able to document results and recognize those who contribute to this success. This first step, although simple, has created a quality awareness among the maintenance personnel which, if further cultivated, will provide dramatic improvements in the services provided to all building occupants. From their experience, management believes the keys to successfully implementing TQM include:

- Keep it simple;
- Involve all levels of the organization;
- Coach rather than manage the process;
- Quickly implement suggestions for change;
- Publish results;
- Give recognition to participants; and
- Repeat process regularly.

DURATION:

Two years.

**TOTAL QUALITY MANAGEMENT
PROCEDURES**

Introduction

Weekly, a representative sampling of completed work orders should be taken by the assigned maintenance manager or supervisor. A suggested sample of 3 - 5% of total work orders for the week is recommended, a minimum of 10 is required. For each of the selected work order(s), the manager/supervisor is to complete the TQM work request questionnaire. There are twelve "yes/no/not applicable" questions and space for appropriate comments and follow-up actions. Follow-up comments should be documented for each "no" answer. If appropriate, a work order should be generated in the maintenance management system.

Example:

	No	Yes
9. Was the area or equipment left clean upon completion?	☑	☐

Comment: John to follow-up with Darrell to get old filters removed from mechanical room.

Upon completion of the TQM work questionnaire, the "Yes's", "No's" and "N/A's" are noted at the bottom of the form. This information is then transferred to the weekly tally sheet. Total the tally sheet and indicate TQM rating. This number is then plotted on the TQM graph and posted in the maintenance area.

Follow-up items are to be reviewed with the maintenance person who completed the work. Action should be taken to prevent items from recurring, i.e., changes in procedures, training, improved communications.

TQM results are to be shared with all maintenance personnel at regular meetings. Follow-up items or trends which are recurring should be discussed and suggestions from maintenance personnel encouraged. TQM results are also to be included in the Manager's Monthly Report as totals and in graph form.

FACILITY MANAGEMENT SERVICES

TOTAL QUALITY MANAGEMENT

MAINTENANCE REQUEST QUESTIONNAIRE

Work Order # _____   Completed By: _____   Reviewing Supervisor: _____

		No	Yes	N/A
1.	Was the work request processed and given to the maintenance person in a timely manner?	☐	☐	☐
	Comments: _____			
2.	Was the appropriate information to complete work requested recorded on work order (including time, requester and requester phone number)?	☐	☐	☐
	Comments: _____			
3.	Did the request get completed within an acceptable time frame?	☐	☐	☐
	Comments: _____			
4.	Were materials necessary readily available to complete request?	☐	☐	☐
	Comments: _____			
5.	Were proper parts/material used in completing job?	☐	☐	☐
	Comments: _____			
6.	Was request completed within acceptable time period?	☐	☐	☐
	Comments: _____			
7.	Was request completed to requester's satisfaction (if possible, talk to requester)?	☐	☐	☐
	Comments: _____			
8.	Was work completed done properly and all necessary follow-up actions taken?	☐	☐	☐
	Comments: _____			
9.	Was area and/or equipment left clean upon completion?	☐	☐	☐
	Comments: _____			
10.	Were proper safety measures applied (safety glass, lockout, _)?	☐	☐	☐
	Comments: _____			
11.	Were all appropriate areas of work order filled out (time, work description, materials, signed)?	☐	☐	☐
	Comments: _____			
12.	Was work order completed/closed out in the maintenance management system?	☐	☐	☐
	Comments: _____			

		No	Yes	N/A
Record Totals on Weekly Tally Form	TOTALS			

Landis & Gyr Powers, Inc. Facility Management Services

BEST PRACTICE

TITLE:

CUSTOMER SATISFACTION PROGRAM

CONTACT:

Mr. Fred J. Klammt
Aptek Associates
625 Ellis Street
Suite 102
Mountain View, CA
94043

415-969-3800

Ms. Francene M. Edeson
Manager of Regional
Building Services
Southern California Edison
PO Box 410
Long Beach, CA 90802

310-491-2751

SUMMARY:

Southern California Edison in Long Beach, California conducted identical survey questionnaires in person and anonymously through the mail without any significant statistical variance between the two methods. Although the in-person surveys did receive immediate feedback on low scores while it was on the customer's mind, the mail-in surveys had similar comment areas filled in for low scores. Southern California Edison expected to find a more favorable bias toward the facilities department when the surveys were done in person by facilities personnel. This was not the case.

BENEFITS:

Other companies which may not have the resources to conduct in-person surveys can adopt this practice, thereby saving resources and having a high degree of certainty of getting valid results. This does not substitute for in-person initial interviews where customers drove the issues that developed the actual survey questions. Cost benefits were reduction in labor resources to conduct a survey and immediate payback for the facilities department. Quality benefits were high confidence in anonymous responses.

LIMITS:

Making certain that return-by-mail questionnaires are returned.

MEASUREMENTS:

- Customer satisfaction matrix scoring (importance and satisfaction);
- Customer satisfaction index (CSI); and
- Cost of survey/customer.

DURATION:

As long as the customer satisfaction program is ongoing.

BEST PRACTICE

TITLE:

DISPOSING OF FURNITURE AND EQUIPMENT: GENERATING GOOD PUBLIC RELATIONS FOR THE FM DEPARTMENT

CONTACT:

Dave Cotts, Chief
Building Maintenance and Repair
The World Bank
1909 K St., NW
Washington, DC 20006

202-458-1966

SUMMARY:

An organization accumulates furniture and office technology which becomes excess to its needs, yet is not economically resalable. One way to dispose of them is to donate them to schools, churches or other charitable organizations. They can also be auctioned off within the company.

BENEFITS:

- Good public or internal relations; and
- Much old equipment and furniture actually "costs" money each time it is handled, therefore making it more cost-effective to dispose of this way.

LIMITS:

- Sensitive programs and information should be removed from office technology before disposal;
- Auctions should be "cash and carry." Auction administration can be a substantial cost; and
- Whatever disposal method is used, minimize your handling of the furniture and equipment or it will become costly.

MEASUREMENTS:

No formal surveys were taken, but The World Bank's External Relations Department has been very pleased with the publicity from the giveaways to local charities. Employees have been very enthusiastic about auctions, particularly "silent auctions."

DURATION:

Frequency is determined by the amount of material accumulated, but an FM organization can reasonably expect to do the above once per year, perhaps in conjunction with Facilities Day.

BEST PRACTICE

TITLE:

COMMUNICATING WITH CUSTOMERS

CONTACT:

Dave Cotts, Chief
Building Maintenance and Repair
The World Bank
1909 K St., NW
Washington, DC 20006

202-458-1966

SUMMARY:

The FM department has established multi-level communications with the employees of The World Bank. The following approaches are suggested:

- Use E-mail. The World Bank's system has the capability to highlight special messages/events.
- Establish an "FM Corner" in the company newsletter to emphasize initiatives or accomplishments or to request support for certain initiatives.
- Use desk-to-desk hotline messages for special events such as an upcoming electrical outage.
- Gain attention in whatever medium you use:
  - Don't be afraid to use some humor;
  - Write well; and
  - Try using an occasional contest to keep up interest in FM communications, e.g., first individual reading the "FM notes" on E-mail calls and receives a plant.

BENEFITS:

- Communications about facility matters is enhanced;
- Users will ultimately decide success or failure so it is in the FM department's best interest to keep them

informed; and

- This type of communication puts a human face on the FM department.

LIMITS:

The message and the messenger must be kept fresh or they just get lost along with all of the other information which bombards your users. No one message or media works all of the time.

MEASUREMENTS:

Customers will tell you how they feel about this type of communication. If you find that they are not responding, then it is time to make a change and vary the medium.

DURATION:

Ongoing.

BEST PRACTICES

TITLE:

AN INTERIORS PREVENTIVE MAINTENANCE CREW

CONTACT:

Dave Cotts, Chief
Building Maintenance and Repair
The World Bank
1909 K St., NW
Washington, DC 20006

202-458-1966

SUMMARY:

   A crew of handymen, easily identified, go through all occupied space on a periodic basis correcting and reporting facility deficiencies. The crew also establishes direct contact with the staff and is the "eyes and ears" of the FM department. Both one and two man teams have been tried: one is the most efficient, two man teams the most effective. A team is kept in a building so that they know the building systems, furniture and finishes, and is changed only after about two years to provide a change in environment and keep the concept fresh. When the team enters a new area, the handyman contacts the head administrative person, socializes a bit and asks about known FM problems. The individual also asks about the deficiencies in executive offices. Policy has been established on what level of facility deficiency the preventive maintenance team can repair and what they must report. Deficiencies which cannot be fixed are turned into a Service Reception Center and converted to service orders.   The most experienced maintenance mechanics on the workforce are used as team members. This team also serves as an excellent "flying squad" for emergencies. The team also inspects special areas such as cafeterias, lobbies, executive areas, conferences facilities, etc. on special cycles (daily, weekly, etc.).

BENEFITS:

- The facilities immediately began to look better;
- After an initial upswing, the service orders reported to the Service Reception Center dropped off; and
- A bond has been cemented between the FM department and its users.

LIMITS:

Guidelines need to be set or the team will get bogged down trying to repair deficiencies which would be more appropriately handled by a specialized crew. They need parameters within which to work.

MEASUREMENTS:

- An excellent program in a large, primarily office space environment to run facilities for $.01/sq. ft./month;
- One man should be able to cover 40-50,000 sq. ft./month; and
- Customer feedback is obtained on survey cards.

DURATION:

This is an ongoing activity in all The World Bank's buildings.

BEST PRACTICE

TITLE:

Periodic Facilities Event

CONTACT:

Dave Cotts, Chief
Building Maintenance and Repair
The World Bank
1909 K St., NW
Washington, DC 20006

202-458-1966

SUMMARY:

About once per year, the FM department sponsors a facilities event, which publicizes the department, emphasizes their programs and contributes to their marketing strategy. The following events have been used:

- Silent auction of excess furniture and office equipment;
- Everyone comes in casual clothes and does painting or touch up work in their areas supported by FM staff;
- A scheduled turn-in of excess furniture and equipment event;
- A recycling booth explaining the advantages and the mechanics of how it will work;
- A trash clean-up day with extra large dumpsters placed strategically throughout the buildings;
- Displaying the outstanding performance of the department with a display in the cafeteria; and
- Intra-department or company-wide games like a packing box deployment relay, timed mail sorting. The FM department gives small prizes for these efforts.

BENEFITS:

The FM department's image as being a contributor to the business and customer friendly has been enhanced. This also is an excellent way to teach users how to access FM services. It is a good way for FM staff to be innovative and creative in developing events.

LIMITS:

The difficult part was getting the first event going. Management was reluctant to support such an activity even though the work benefits are great. People are reluctant to participate because they do not think they should spare the time to be involved. FM management had to be careful that the prizes did not get out of control and become too expensive.

MEASUREMENTS:

The best measure is the participation and feedback from customers. They also learn something about FM services and find the event both enjoyable and helpful.

DURATION:

Probably no more than once per year.

BEST PRACTICES

TITLE:

USING A TQM CONCEPT IN RIGHTSIZING A FACILITIES ORGANIZATION

CONTACT:

Ms. Stormy Friday
President
The Friday Group
1215 Cameron Street
Alexandria, VA 22314

703-548-5697

SUMMARY:

In developing a reorganization plan for the Office of Headquarters Services (OHS) of a government organization, The Friday Group used the Total Quality Management (TQM) concept of an interactive group process session. Thirty people representing a cross section of the organization from the housekeeping to space management staff met for a day-long reorganization workshop. In the morning small break-out groups were asked to be introspective about the current organization and to:

- Identify services currently provided within each organizational unit;
- Identify contracts managed within each organizational unit; and
- Identify problems they had in providing current services which were attributed to the total OHS organization.

Each group selected a facilitator from within the group and a group member to report back to the large group on their findings.

In the afternoon the break-out groups concentrated on a new organization. A straw model was provided and they were asked to focus on:

- A definition of the new organization unit;
- How they would organize a staff to provide the services identified;
- The types of staff expertise they needed to add to the organization unit to strengthen it; and
- Additional suggestions about the total new OHS organization.

BENEFITS:

- The TQM concept of empowering staff was exemplified. The staff had an opportunity to have direct input into the way the organization would be shaped. In effect, they were controlling their own destiny;
- The workshop diffused underlying apprehension about the purpose of the reorganization. OHS staff became part of the process and could "buy in" to the reorganization effort;
- The consultants obtained valuable data which reduced the level of effort required to collect background information (on contracts, services, etc.); and
- A facilities organization (OHS) gained recognition as a leader in the agency's TQM effort.

LIMITS:

Top management must endorse and participate in the process.

MEASUREMENTS:

- Many ideas regarding new procedures and practices for services which came out of the workshop were implemented immediately. OHS customers saw improvement in service;
- Morale of OHS staff improved tremendously. Staff were excited about the reorganization;
- Much of what the break-out groups recommended was incorporated into the final organization plan. OHS staff realized the results of their efforts.

DURATION:

The reorganization workshop concept has been in practice in the agency for one year. The Friday Group uses the workshop concept in all facility organization assessment projects.

BEST PRACTICES

TITLE:

Creating a Space Committee to Make Organizational Decisions Regarding Space Within the Quality Management Framework

CONTACT:

Ms. Stormy Friday	Ms. Gayle Silva
President	Project Administrator
The Friday Group	Information Resources
1215 Cameron Street	Management Service (IRMS)
Alexandria, VA 22314	General Services
	Administration
	18th and F Streets, NW
	Washington, DC 20405
703-548-5697	202-501-1197

SUMMARY:

In 1991, The Friday Group conducted a study and developed a master space plan for IRMS. The study concluded that IRMS had a space shortfall and required the acquisition of additional space. Based on the findings and recommendations of the study, the Commissioner of IRMS established a Space Committee to:

- Develop and recommend IRMS-wide space and furniture guidelines;
- Investigate and recommend alternative file/record storage and retrieval systems;
- Investigate and recommend conference room alternatives; and
- Develop and recommend a backfill plan for space vacated by an IRMS component moving outside the building.

The Committee consisted of decision makers from each of the IRMS Offices and adopted the approach of a Process Action Team to carry out the Commissioner's charge. Using a facilitated process, the Committee:

- Formulated overarching guidelines designed to:
  - Provide for minimal disruption to Offices;
  - Consider recent renovations;
  - Control costs; and
  - Give every Office some additional space.
- Directed The Friday Group to conduct an analysis and develop alternatives consistent with the overarching guidelines; and
- Evaluated the alternatives and developed recommendations for an IRMS-wide implementation and backfill plan.

BENEFITS:

1. All members of the Committee put aside vested interests for additional space to determine what was best for the IRMS organization as a whole.
2. The Committee established policies and procedures for future space requests and distribution.
3. The Committee is viewed as the organization decision maker with respect to all space matters.   No decision regarding space (e.g. alterations, changes in electrical/mechanical/telephone closets, etc.) can be made without review and approval by the Committee.
4. All Offices have a forum to air their needs, concerns and issues.

LIMITS:

The process must be facilitated until the group is able to self-facilitate on a regular basis.

MEASUREMENTS:

- The ability of the Committee to be proactive rather than reactive;
- Acceptance of plans and recommendations by Senior Management of IRMS;
- Institutionalization of the Committee as the space oversight group; and

- Development of an annual space and furniture plan for IRMS.

DURATION:

The Space Committee has been in effect for two years. It provided oversight on the implementation of the backfill plan and addressed new requirements for additional space.

APPENDIX

USING IFMA'S STANDARDIZED FACILITY MANAGEMENT CUSTOMER SATISFACTION QUESTIONNAIRE

BACKGROUND

IFMA has designed and pretested a standardized questionnaire for measuring and tracking employee satisfaction with the services provided by facility management. The questionnaire is designed to measure satisfaction both with how the facility is managed, and with interacting with the facility management staff.

There are two ways to use this questionnaire to conduct a tracking survey:
1. You can administer it in its standardized form to employees; or
2. You can use it as a starting point for creating your own questionnaire.

The advantage to using the standardized questionnaire is that by supplying a summary of results to IFMA, you can receive benchmarking data from other IFMA members.

HOW TO ADMINISTER THE STANDARDIZED FORM

The following instructions should be followed for conducting an employee survey using the standardized IFMA customer satisfaction questionnaire:

1. Sampling:
It is not necessary to include all employees in your survey. Using the following scale, determine how many employees to include in your sample.

Number of employees at a site:	Percent who should receive questionnaire
200 or less	100%
201-500	50% or more
501-1000	40% or more
1001-2000	30% or more
Over 2000	20% or more

If you are not going to include all employees in the survey, those who will participate should be chosen at random. Ideally, your human resources department can generate a list of randomly-selected employee names. For example, if there are 2000 employees at a given site, you will need to select 400 names at random from the list of employees at that site. This can be done by by selecting a random starting point at the beginning of the list, then selecting every fifth employee name after that point.

If you do not have the capability of selecting employees at random, another option is to select work units or departments at random, and survey all employees in the selected departments. Contact IFMA for assistance with this approach.

2. Questionnaire:
While you are having your list drawn, duplicate the questionnaire. Please note that Importance ratings are included in each section. You may find these responses useful for planning purposes; however, this information is not reported to or tracked by IFMA.

3. Cover letter:
Write a memo or cover letter to attach to each questionnaire explaining the purpose of the survey. Make sure to include:
1. An explanation of how the results will be used.
2. That the respondent's name was chosen at random.
3. That the form is not signed, and the results will be kept confidential.
4. A deadline for returning the form (allow two weeks.)
5. Instructions on where and how to return the form.

4. Distributing questionnaires:

It is strongly recommended that questionnaires be sent to employees at their office or work location, rather than at home. Using company time to complete the survey will result in much higher response rates. You should try to receive at least 30% of the questionnaires back from employees. Sending reminder cards, voice mail messages and other communications will help increase your response level.

5. Tabulating the survey:

After you receive all of the completed questionnaires, tally the responses to each question. You can use the attached reporting form to record both the frequency with which each number was circled for each Satisfaction question, and the average rating for each question.

By returning your reporting form to IFMA, you will receive benchmarking data on the survey.

If desired, IFMA can tabulate your questionnaires for an additional charge.

For additional assistance or questions, please contact IFMA at (713) 623-4362.

FACILITY MANAGEMENT CUSTOMER SATISFACTION SURVEY

Your feedback is crucial in improving the quality of services provided by the facility management staff. Facility management is responsible for things like space planning, heating and cooling, telecommunications, maintenance and other operations of the physical plant, as well as security, food service and other types of administrative services related to operating the facility.

Please circle the number next to each statement which best reflects your level of satisfaction with facility management at your site. If for any reason you decide not to answer a question, circle "6" under N/A (No Answer). Use the "Comments" space to give more information about areas in which you feel dissatisfied.

BACKGROUND

These questions are for grouping purposes only. Please circle the number which best represents your major job function, or "Other" if your responsibilities fall outside the areas listed.

Executive	1	Technical Specialist	4
Manager/Supervisor	2	Clerical	5
Administrative	3	Other	6

How often do you interact with the Facility Management Department?

More than once a week	1	4-6 times per year	4
About two times a month	2	Once or twice a year	5
About once a month	3	Never	6

Gender:

Male	1	Female	2

Length of time at your present location:

Less than one year	1	6-10 years	4
1-2 years	2	Over 10 years	5
3-5 years	3		

1 FACILITY MANAGEMENT STAFF

Please indicate your level of *satisfaction* with your Facility Management Staff by circling the appropriate number for each characteristic listed. Also, please indicate how *important* each of these characteristics are to you by circling the appropriate number.

	SATISFACTION						IMPORTANCE					
	Very Dissatisfied			Very Satisfied		N/A	Not Very Important			Very Important		N/A
Technical competence	1	2	3	4	5	6	1	2	3	4	5	6
Knowledge of the building and building systems	1	2	3	4	5	6	1	2	3	4	5	6
Availability	1	2	3	4	5	6	1	2	3	4	5	6
Trustworthiness	1	2	3	4	5	6	1	2	3	4	5	6
Timeliness of response	1	2	3	4	5	6	1	2	3	4	5	6
Appearance	1	2	3	4	5	6	1	2	3	4	5	6
Courtesy	1	2	3	4	5	6	1	2	3	4	5	6
Understanding your needs/requirements	1	2	3	4	5	6	1	2	3	4	5	6

Overall, how satisfied are you with your facility management staff?

1	2	3	4	5	6

Comments:

2 YOUR BUILDING AND OFFICE ENVIRONMENT

Please indicate your level of *satisfaction* with your building and office environment by circling the appropriate number for each component listed. Also, please indicate how *important* each of these components are to you by circling the appropriate number.

	SATISFACTION						IMPORTANCE					
	Very Dissatisfied			Very Satisfied		N/A	Not Very Important			Very Important		N/A
Location	1	2	3	4	5	6	1	2	3	4	5	6
Availability of parking	1	2	3	4	5	6	1	2	3	4	5	6
Availability of public transportation	1	2	3	4	5	6	1	2	3	4	5	6
Security	1	2	3	4	5	6	1	2	3	4	5	6
Attractiveness of appearance	1	2	3	4	5	6	1	2	3	4	5	6
Grounds/Landscaping	1	2	3	4	5	6	1	2	3	4	5	6
Signs (for directions around the facility)	1	2	3	4	5	6	1	2	3	4	5	6
Temperature	1	2	3	4	5	6	1	2	3	4	5	6
Lighting	1	2	3	4	5	6	1	2	3	4	5	6
Noise level	1	2	3	4	5	6	1	2	3	4	5	6
Indoor air quality	1	2	3	4	5	6	1	2	3	4	5	6
Furniture	1	2	3	4	5	6	1	2	3	4	5	6
Interior layout	1	2	3	4	5	6	1	2	3	4	5	6
Telephone system	1	2	3	4	5	6	1	2	3	4	5	6
Voice mail system	1	2	3	4	5	6	1	2	3	4	5	6
Handicapped accessibility	1	2	3	4	5	6	1	2	3	4	5	6
Restrooms	1	2	3	4	5	6	1	2	3	4	5	6
Lounge/Common areas	1	2	3	4	5	6	1	2	3	4	5	6
If available:												
Child care facilities	1	2	3.	4	5	6	1	2	3	4	5	6
Fitness center	1	2	3	4	5	6	1	2	3	4	5	6
Snack bar/Food service	1	2	3	4	5	6	1	2	3	4	5	6

Overall, how satisfied are you with your building and office environment?

.... 1   2   3   4   5   6

Comments:

_____

_____

_____

3 BUILDING EQUIPMENT

Please indicate your level of *satisfaction* with the quality of your building equipment by circling the appropriate number for each factor listed. Also, please indicate how *important* each of these factors are to you by circling the appropriate number.

	SATISFACTION						IMPORTANCE					
	Very Dissatisfied			Very Satisfied		N/A	Not Very Important			Very Important		N/A
Elevators	1	2	3	4	5	6	1	2	3	4	5	6
Escalators	1	2	3	4	5	6	1	2	3	4	5	6
Plumbing	1	2	3	4	5	6	1	2	3	4	5	6
Heating	1	2	3	4	5	6	1	2	3	4	5	6
Air conditioning	1	2	3	4	5	6	1	2	3	4	5	6
Ventilation	1	2	3	4	5	6	1	2	3	4	5	6

Overall, how satisfied are you with your building equipment?

.... 1   2   3   4   5   6

Comments:

_____

_____

_____

4 BUILDING SERVICES

Please indicate your level of *satisfaction* with the services provided by the Facility Management department by circling the appropriate number for each service listed. Also, please indicate how *important* each of these services are to you by circling the appropriate number.

	SATISFACTION						IMPORTANCE					
	Very Dissatisfied			Very Satisfied		N/A	Not Very Important			Very Important		N/A
Quality of:												
Cleaning	1	2	3	4	5	6	1	2	3	4	5	6
Maintenance	1	2	3	4	5	6	1	2	3	4	5	6
Repairs	1	2	3	4	5	6	1	2	3	4	5	6
Alterations	1	2	3	4	5	6	1	2	3	4	5	6
Timeliness of:												
Maintenance	1	2	3	4	5	6	1	2	3	4	5	6
Repairs	1	2	3	4	5	6	1	2	3	4	5	6
Frequency of cleaning	1	2	3	4	5	6	1	2	3	4	5	6

Overall, how satisfied are you with the building services described above?

| | 1 | 2 | 3 | 4 | 5 | 6 |

Comments:

_____
_____
_____

5 PROCEDURES

Please indicate your level of *satisfaction* with the procedures you must go through in order to obtain service from the Facility Management department by circling the appropriate number for each characteristic listed. Also, please indicate how *important* each of these characteristics are to you by circling the appropriate number.

	SATISFACTION						IMPORTANCE					
	Very Dissatisfied			Very Satisfied		N/A	Not Very Important			Very Important		N/A
Ease of doing business	1	2	3	4	5	6	1	2	3	4	5	6
Accommodation of unique requirements	1	2	3	4	5	6	1	2	3	4	5	6
Flexibility	1	2	3	4	5	6	1	2	3	4	5	6
Responsiveness	1	2	3	4	5	6	1	2	3	4	5	6
Effectiveness of communications	1	2	3	4	5	6	1	2	3	4	5	6

Overall, how satisfied are you with procedures for obtaining services from the Facility Management department?

| | 1 | 2 | 3 | 4 | 5 | 6 |

Comments:

_____
_____
_____

6 OVERALL SATISFACTION RATING

Overall, how satisfied are you with the services provided by your facility management staff?

SATISFACTION					
Very Dissatisfied			Very Satisfied		N/A
1	2	3	4	5	6

Comments:

_____
_____

IFMA REPORTING FORM FOR CUSTOMER SATISFACTION SURVEY

BACKGROUND QUESTIONS

What is the total number of employees at site/building for which survey was conducted? _____

How many surveys did you distribute? _____

How many responses did you receive? _____

Please put the number of respondents in your sample for each major job function.

_____ Executive
_____ Manager/Supervisor
_____ Administrative
_____ Technical Specialist
_____ Clerical
_____ Other

Please indicate the number of respondents which checked each category below in response to "How often do you interact with the Facility Management Department?"

_____ More than once a week
_____ About two times a month
_____ About once a month
_____ 4-6 times per year
_____ Once or twice a year
_____ Never

Please indicate the number of respondents in each gender category.

_____ Male
_____ Female

Please indicate the number of respondents which checked each category below in response to length of time at present location.

_____ Less than one year   _____ 6-10 years
_____ 1-2 years   _____ over 10 years
_____ 3-5 years

1 FACILITY MANAGEMENT STAFF

Please indicate your level of satisfaction with your Facility Management Staff:
Please list the number of responses you received next to each rating.
Also give your average for each in the space provided.

AVERAGE		<< VERY DISSATISFIED			VERY SATISFIED >>

_____ Technical competence .... 1 _____ 2 _____ 3 _____ 4 _____ 5 _____
_____ Knowledge of the building and building systems ...... 1 _____ 2 _____ 3 _____ 4 _____ 5 _____
_____ Availability .... 1 _____ 2 _____ 3 _____ 4 _____ 5 _____
_____ Trustworthiness .... 1 _____ 2 _____ 3 _____ 4 _____ 5 _____
_____ Timeliness of response .... 1 _____ 2 _____ 3 _____ 4 _____ 5 _____
_____ Appearance... 1 _____ 2 _____ 3 _____ 4 _____ 5 _____
_____ Courtesy.. 1 _____ 2 _____ 3 _____ 4 _____ 5 _____
_____ Understanding of your requirements........................ 1 _____ 2 _____ 3 _____ 4 _____ 5 _____

_____ Overall, how satisfied are you with your facility management staff
.... 1 _____ 2 _____ 3 _____ 4 _____ 5 _____

2 YOUR BUILDING AND OFFICE ENVIRONMENT

Please indicate your level of satisfaction with your building and office environment:
Please list the number of responses you received next to each rating.
Also give your average for each in the space provided.

AVERAGE   **<< VERY DISSATISFIED   VERY SATISFIED >>**

		1	2	3	4	5
_____	Location	1 ____	2 ____	3 ____	4 ____	5 ____
_____	Availability of parking	1 ____	2 ____	3 ____	4 ____	5 ____
_____	Availability of public transportation	1 ____	2 ____	3 ____	4 ____	5 ____
_____	Security	1 ____	2 ____	3 ____	4 ____	5 ____
_____	Attractiveness of appearance	1 ____	2 ____	3 ____	4 ____	5 ____
_____	Grounds/Landscaping	1 ____	2 ____	3 ____	4 ____	5 ____
_____	Signs	1 ____	2 ____	3 ____	4 ____	5 ____
_____	Temperature	1 ____	2 ____	3 ____	4 ____	5 ____
_____	Lighting	1 ____	2 ____	3 ____	4 ____	5 ____
_____	Noise level	1 ____	2 ____	3 ____	4 ____	5 ____
_____	Indoor air quality	1 ____	2 ____	3 ____	4 ____	5 ____
_____	Furniture	1 ____	2 ____	3 ____	4 ____	5 ____
_____	Interior layout	1 ____	2 ____	3 ____	4 ____	5 ____
_____	Telephone system	1 ____	2 ____	3 ____	4 ____	5 ____
_____	Voice mail system	1 ____	2 ____	3 ____	4 ____	5 ____
_____	Handicapped accessibility	1 ____	2 ____	3 ____	4 ____	5 ____
_____	Restrooms	1 ____	2 ____	3 ____	4 ____	5 ____
_____	Lounge/Common areas	1 ____	2 ____	3 ____	4 ____	5 ____
_____	Child care facilities	1 ____	2 ____	3 ____	4 ____	5 ____
_____	Fitness center	1 ____	2 ____	3 ____	4 ____	5 ____
_____	Snack bar/Food services	1 ____	2 ____	3 ____	4 ____	5 ____

_____ Overall, how satisfied are you with your building and office environment
.... 1 ____ 2 ____ 3 ____ 4 ____ 5 ____

3 BUILDING EQUIPMENT

Please indicate your level of satisfaction with the quality of your building equipment:
Please list the number of responses you received next to each rating.
Also give your average for each in the space provided.

AVERAGE   **<< VERY DISSATISFIED   VERY SATISFIED >>**

		1	2	3	4	5
_____	Elevators	1 ____	2 ____	3 ____	4 ____	5 ____
_____	Escalators	1 ____	2 ____	3 ____	4 ____	5 ____
_____	Plumbing	1 ____	2 ____	3 ____	4 ____	5 ____
_____	Heating	1 ____	2 ____	3 ____	4 ____	5 ____
_____	Air conditioning	1 ____	2 ____	3 ____	4 ____	5 ____
_____	Ventilation	1 ____	2 ____	3 ____	4 ____	5 ____

_____ Overall, how satisfied are you with your building equipment
.... 1 ____ 2 ____ 3 ____ 4 ____ 5 ____

4 BUILDING SERVICES

Please indicate your level of satisfaction with the services provided by the Facility Management department:
Please list the number of responses you received next to each rating.
Also give your average for each in the space provided.

| AVERAGE | | << VERY DISSATISFIED | | | VERY SATISFIED >> |

Quality of:

_____ Cleaning .... 1 _____ 2 _____ 3 _____ 4 _____ 5 _____
_____ Maintenance.................................. 1 _____ 2 _____ 3 _____ 4 _____ 5 _____
_____ Repairs... 1 _____ 2 _____ 3 _____ 4 _____ 5 _____
_____ Alterations .... 1 _____ 2 _____ 3 _____ 4 _____ 5 _____

Timeliness of:

_____ Maintenance.................................. 1 _____ 2 _____ 3 _____ 4 _____ 5 _____
_____ Repairs... 1 _____ 2 _____ 3 _____ 4 _____ 5 _____

_____ Frequency of cleaning .... 1 _____ 2 _____ 3 _____ 4 _____ 5 _____

_____ Overall, how satisfied are you with the building services described above
.... 1 _____ 2 _____ 3 _____ 4 _____ 5 _____

5 PROCEDURES

Please indicate the level of satisfaction with the procedures you must go through in order to obtain services from the Facility Management department:
Please list the number of responses you received next to each rating.
Also give your average for each in the space provided.

| AVERAGE | | << VERY DISSATISFIED | | | VERY SATISFIED >> |

_____ Ease of doing business .... 1 _____ 2 _____ 3 _____ 4 _____ 5 _____
_____ Accommodation of unique requirements .... 1 _____ 2 _____ 3 _____ 4 _____ 5 _____
_____ Flexibility .... 1 _____ 2 _____ 3 _____ 4 _____ 5 _____
_____ Responsiveness.............................. 1 _____ 2 _____ 3 _____ 4 _____ 5 _____
_____ Effectiveness of communications .... 1 _____ 2 _____ 3 _____ 4 _____ 5 _____

_____ Overall, how satisfied are you with procedures for obtaining services from the facility management
department....................................... 1 _____ 2 _____ 3 _____ 4 _____ 5 _____

6 OVERALL SATISFACTION RATING

Overall, how satisfied are you with the services provided by your Facility Management staff?

| AVERAGE | | << VERY DISSATISFIED | | | VERY SATISFIED >> |

Please list the number of responses you received next to each rating.
1 _____ 2 _____ 3 _____ 4 _____ 5 _____

What is your average (mean) overall rating?_____

BIBLIOGRAPHY

Albrecht, Karl. *The Only Thing that Matters: Bringing the Power of the Customer into the Center of Your Business*. New York: Harper Business, 1992.

Band, William A. *Creating Value for Customers: Designing and Implementing a Total Corporate Strategy*. New York: John Wiley & Sons, Inc., 1991.

Bers, Joanna Smith. "Kennametal's, Gregory: An FM Marketing Maverick." *Facilities Design & Management* (March 1994), 44-47

Bowen, David E. and Lawlers, Edward E., III. "The Empowerment of Service Workers: What, Why, How and When." *Sloan Management Review*, 33 # 3 (Spring 1992), 31-39.

Bowles, Jerry. "Is American Management Really Committed to QUALITY?" *Management Review* (April 1992), 42-46.

Camp, Robert C. *Benchmarking*. Milwaukee, Wisconsin, ASQC Quality Press, 1989.

Carr, David K. and Littman, Ian D. *Excellence in Government: Total Quality Management in the 1990s*. Arlington, Virginia: Coopers & Lybrand, 1990.

Chapman, Robert L. *Dictionary of American Slang*. New York: Harper and Row, 1986.

Cohen, William A. *The Art of the Leader*. Englewood Cliffs, New Jersey: Prentice Hall, 1990.

Cotts, David G. and Lee, Michael. *The Facility Management Handbook*. New York: AMACOM, 1992.

Crosby, Philip B. *Quality Without Tears: The Art of Hassel-Free Management*. New York: McGraw-Hill, 1984.

Crosby, Philip B. "The 21st Century Leadership." *Journal for Quality and Participation* (July/August 1992).

Crosby, Philip B. *Leading, The Art of Becoming an Executive*. New York: McGraw-Hill, 1990.

Customer Focus Research, Executive Briefing. Boston, Massachusetts: The Forum Corporation, 1988.

Deming, William Edwards. *Out of Crisis*. Cambridge, Massachusetts: MIT Center for Advanced Engineering Study, 1986.

Denton, Keith D. *Horizontal Management: Beyond Total Customer Satisfaction*. New York: Lexington Books, Macmillian, Inc., 1991.

Dwyer, Paula. "The New Gospel of Good Government." *Business Week* (January 20, 1992).

Elders, Alvin. "QM for FMs: Can Total Quality Management Programs Make a Difference?" *Today's Facility Manager* (October 1993), 1 and 4-43.

"From Top Secret to Top Priority: The Story of TQM," *Aviation Week & Space Technology* (May 21, 1990), 57-524

Hart, Christopher W.L., Hiskett, James L. and Susser, Earl W. Jr. "The Profitable Art of Service Recovery," *Harvard Business Review* (July-August, 1990).

Hinton, Thomas D. *The Spirit of Service: How to Create a Customer-Focused Service Culture: A Customer Service Strategy for the New Decade and Beyond*. Dubuque, Iowa: Kendall/Hunt Publishing, 1991.

"Human Resources." *Facility Management Journal* (September/October 1991).

Hutchins, Greg. *Purchasing Strategies for Total Quality: A Guide to Achieving Continuous Improvement.* Homewood, Illinois: Business One Irwin, 1992.

Hyde, Albert C. "Feedback from Customers, Clients and Captives." *The Bureaucrat* (Winter 1991/92).

Ishikawa, Kaoru. *Guide to Quality Control.* White Plains, New York: Quality Resources Press, 1986.

Juran, J.M. *Juran on Quality by Design: The New Steps for Planning Quality into Goods and Services.* New York: The Free Press, 1992.

Juran, J.M. *Managerial Breakthrough – A New Concept of the Manager's Job.* New York: McGraw-Hill, 1964.

Kinlaw, Dennis C. *Developing Superior Work Teams: Building Quality and the Competitive Edge.* Lexington, Massachusetts: Lexington Books, 1991.

Kouzes, James M. and Posner, Barry Z. "The Credibility Factor: What Followers Expect from Their Leaders." *Management Review* (January 1990).

Kouzes, James M. and Posner, Barry Z. *The Leadership Challenge: How to Get Extraordinary Things Done in Organizations.* San Francisco: Josey-Buss Publishers, 1989.

Lash, Linda M. *The Complete Guide to Customer Service.* New York: John Wiley & Sons, Inc., 1989.

Leibfried, Kathleen H.J. and McNair, C.J. *Benchmarking: A Tool for Continuous Improvement.* New York: Harper Collins Publishers, Inc., 1992.

Leswood, Laurce A. "A New System for Rating Service Quality," Source Unknown.

Levesque, Paul. "Having Fun with Quality Management." *Quality Digest* (September 1991).

Lynch, Barry. "Making Measurement Activities Produce Results." *The Facility Management Journal* (July/August 1993).

Lynch, Richard L. and Cross, Kalvin F. *Measure Up! Yardsticks for Continuous Improvement.* Cambridge, Massachusetts: Basil Blackwell, 1991.

"Management Practices: U.S. Companies Improve Performance Through Quality Efforts." *A Report to the Honorable Donald Ritter. House of Representatives.* Washington, DC: U.S. General Accounting Office, May 1991.

Mumford, Steve. "Managing Total Quality: Improving Facilities Departments from Within." *Corporate Facilities* (March 1993), 31-32.

Neldon, Christine N. "Quality: A Crucial Concept for Facility Managers." *Modern Office Technology* (June 1991), 62-64.

Osborne, David and Gaebler, Ted. *Reinventing Government: How the Entrepreneurial Spirit is Transforming the Public Sector.* Reading, Massachusetts: Addison-Wesley, 1992.

Paton, Scott Madison. "Is Quality Dead?" *Quality Digest* (April 1994).

Peters, (Tom) Thomas J. *Thriving on Chaos: Handbook for a Management Revolution.* New York: Harper & Row, 1988.

Peters, Tom. *In Search of Excellence.* New York: Harper & Row, 1982.

"Quality Programs in Facility Management." *Research Report #9.* Houston, Texas: International Facility Management Association, 1992.

"Quality." *Facility Management Journal* (July/August 1993).

"Recipe for Successful Facilities Management." *Modern Office Technology* (June 1991), 29-34.

Reynolds, Gary (editor). *Building Quality: TQM for Campus Facilities Managers.* Alexandria, Virginia: Association of Higher Education Facilities Officers, 1994.

Reynolds, Gary. "Total Quality Management for Campus Facilities." *Facilities Manager* (Summer 1992), 14-20.

Russel, J.P. *Quality Management Benchmark Assessment*. Milwaukee, Wisconsin: ASQC Quality Press, 1991.

Schultes, Peter R. *The Team Handbook: How to Use Teams to Improve Quality*. Madison, Wisconsin: Joiner Associates, Inc., 1988.

Sellerman, Saul W. *Management by Motivation*. New York: American Management Association, Inc., 1969.

"Some Thoughts at the Outset: Joseph Juran on Bringing TQM to Government." *The GAO Journal* (Winter 1991/92).

"Strategic Planning." *Facility Management Journal* (October 1989).

Total Quality Management: An Overview Student Manual. Washington, DC: General Services Administration, GSA Training Center, 1990.

"Total Quality Management: What's It All About! Is It Right For Your Company?" *Today's Facility Manager* (June 1993), 1, 19 and 27.

Varian, Tom, "Communicating Total Quality Inside the Organization." *Quality Progress*, 24 #6 (June 1991), 30-31.

Walton, May. *The Deming Management Method*. New York: Putnam, 1986.

Webster's New Collegiate Dictionary, Eighth Edition.

Wellins, Richard S. *Empowered Teams: Creating Self-Directed Work Groups That Improve Quality, Productivity and Participation*. San Francisco: Jossey-Bass, 1991.

Zeithaml, Valerie A., Parasuraman, A. and Berry, Leonard L. *Delivering Quality Services: Balancing Customer Perceptions and Expectations*. New York: The Free Press, 1990.

Zemke, Ron. "Auditing Customer Service: Look Inside as Well as Out." *Employment Relations Today* (Autumn 1989), 197-203.

Zemke, Ron. "Faith, Hope and TQM." *Training* (January 1992), 8.

Zemke, Ron. "The Emerging Art of Service Management." *Training* (January 1992), 37-42.

Zemke, Ron with Schaaf, Dick. *The Service Edge: 101 Companies that Profit from Customer Care.* New York: New American Library, 1989.

INDEX